Dea

THIRTY YEARS OF

RECIPE REQUESTS

TO THE LOS ANGELES TIMES

ROSE DOSTI

❖

Los Angeles Times
A Times Mirror Company

Los Angeles, California

Los Angeles Times

Publisher: Richard T. Schlosberg III
Editor: Shelby Coffey III
Managing Editor: George Cotliar
Associate Editor: Narda Zacchino

Project Director: Angela Rinaldi
Produced by: Bill Dorich, I.P.A. Graphics Management, Inc.
Book Design: Patricia Moritz

Library of Congress Catalogue Number: 94–076758
ISBN 1–883792–06–1
Copyright © 1994, Los Angeles Times

Published by the Los Angeles Times Syndicate
Times Mirror Square, Los Angeles, California 90053
A Times Mirror Company

First printing, August, 1994
Second printing, May 1995
Third printing, August, 1997

Printed in U.S.A

Contents

ACKNOWLEDGEMENTS

❖

Dear S.O.S. owes a debt of gratitude to past and present editors, home economists and Los Angeles Times test-kitchen staff who over thirty years tested, corrected and developed recipes. Anita Bennett, the first editor of the column when it ran in the Daily Mirror, Cecil Fleming, a home economist who succeeded Mrs. Bennett after the Daily Mirror merged with the Los Angeles Times, have a place of honor among those who contributed to the recipes' success. Special thanks go to today's Los Angeles Times test-kitchen staff–Donna Deane, who tested many of the recipes as home economist for the Food Section, assistant Mayi Brady and Anna Oviedo. Several staff members who are now retired must also be acknowledged–thank you Minnie Bernadino, Helen Stefenac and Judy Masters.

INTRODUCTION

❖

In response to the letters we've received from readers of the popular food column *Dear S.O.S.*, which appears weekly in the Los Angeles Times food section, we are delighted to present the first volume of the recipes readers have regularly requested over the last thirty years. These are the favorites that readers write in for over and over again. Recipes from the nostalgic past–a grandmother's pudding or the cookies baked at city school cafeterias, and favorites from the present–Spago's crabcakes or the chicken fajitas from El Torito, a chain of Mexican restaurants.

Dear S.O.S. has a long history. It began as a column in the Los Angeles Times in 1961 but it appeared in The Daily Mirror before that. It's first editor there was Anita Bennett and her audience was mostly homemakers who were curious and innovative, but limited by the foodstuffs found in the markets at that time. From the thirties to the sixties, canned goods were used most frequently in cooking. Fresh fruits and vegetables were almost unheard of out-of-season. Few recipes called for fresh herbs. *Fruit Cocktail Cake* was among the favorites. So was *Mystery Salad*, a gelatin-based salad that was popular on buffet tables. The handful of major restaurants in our area were the only inspiration for the fancy dishes. Many of the original restaurants are now closed–The Brown Derby, Scandia, The Bistro–but the dishes created in those kitchens have become part of Los Angeles' culinary history.

Cecil Fleming was the next editor and her audience, suffering from economic malaise, requested recipes for hard economic times–casseroles and potluck dishes, simple foods based on nostalgia and tight budgets. When I took the column over in the early seventies, the health food movement erupted to create havoc and confusion in food ideas and eating. We created recipes for granola, nut burgers, vegetarian meat loafs and carrot cake. At the same time we printed recipes for such tempting desserts as *Flourless Chocolate* and *Chocolate Cheesecake*.

Requests for recipes throughout the late seventies and eighties reflected a wider taste for variety. The growing ethnic population in Los Angeles was more diverse than any city in the country and contributed to a growing appetite for new and exotic foods. Dishes from the growing Latino, Japanese, Vietnamese and Korean populations suddenly were in demand. As more women joined the work force and home-cooking waned, more requests came for dishes eaten in restaurants than any other type.

A cross-cultural cuisine was created by the influx of professional chefs from other countries. Technological ideas in agriculture, storage and distribution brought overnight delivery of exotic foods from the Continent and Asia. These chefs applied their creative energies to the new ideas and ingredients available to them as never before. Readers eating out fell in love with the dishes created by Celestino Drago, Joachim Splichal and Wolfgang Puck and sent in their requests.

The requests haven't stopped, thousands come in each year. Many of the nostalgic requests are in our files dating as far back as the early forties; while others are sought in cookbooks, letters to chefs, home cooks, restaurants, caterers, the food industry and other sources. In addition to requests readers share their favorite recipes with us. Every recipe has been tested in our test kitchen and many have been developed by our staff home economists.

Dear S.O.S Thirty Years of Recipe Requests to the Los Angeles Times will contain many of your own favorites—if not, our apologies until the next edition.

❖

How To Use Our Recipes

All of the recipes in the book have been tested in our kitchen using the measurements and ingredients specified. If your creativity urges you to make substitutions, and we haven't included any, do so at your own risk, most recipes will not suffer great damage but we cannot guarantee that the recipes will work out. The following notes should be helpful:

❖ Although some recipes call for *uncooked eggs*, the U.S. Department of Agriculture has found them to be a potential carrier of food-borne illness and recommends avoiding eating raw eggs. Commercial egg substitutes may be used in place of raw eggs in certain circumstances. Check egg substitute package for applications.

❖ When you use *eggs*, use large eggs for the recipes. A large egg is equivalent to $\frac{1}{4}$ cup beaten egg. If using jumbo, medium or small eggs, measure.

❖ In *baking*, unless alternative ingredients are given, do not substitute ingredients. One can add dried or fresh herbs, spices, nuts, coconut and other add-ons but tampering with dry and liquid ingredients in baked products may destroy the chemical balance and result in failure.

❖ You can substitute one *liquid* for another, such as juice for water or wine for juice, but avoid changing the amount of liquid called for.

❖ When *oil* is given as an ingredient, use vegetable oil unless another is specified.

❖ Use your own judgement and preferred methods for *blending, mixing, cutting or grinding*. You might want to use a food processor for blending or grinding or an electric mixer with a dough hook to avoid kneading doughs by hand.

❖ *Cooked measurements* are different than uncooked. For example, 1 cup of uncooked noodles will yield more than a cup of cooked noodles.

❖ Use standard *measuring tools*. All measures should be level, not heaping, unless specified.

❖ When *igniting alcoholic liquids*, be cautious. Keep hands, face, dish towels or loose clothing away from the flame. Use extra–long matches or lighter extensions when igniting liquids. Never place wine bottles or other alcoholic beverages near flames. Never pour their contents on food when the food is near a flame.

❖ *Baking temperatures* are expressed in Fahrenheit.

❖ We often refer to chicken as broiler-fryers, weighing $2\frac{1}{2}$ to 3 pounds.

❖ If using *dried herbs*, use a third of the measurements specified for the fresh herb.

❖ When unspecified, *milk* refers to homogenized, pasteurized whole milk. Nonfat milk contains no fat and may be substituted for whole milk in some circumstances. Evaporated milk is used undiluted in recipes unless specified. Do not interchange evaporated milk and sweetened condensed milk.

❖ *Rice* is long-grain regular rice unless specified as converted, short-grain, brown, wild or instant precooked. Follow manufacturers' instructions when cooking rice, particularly instant precooked rice.

❖ When making *pasta*, follow the instructions on the package unless specified. Use a colander to drain, shaking until excess moisture is removed. To keep from sticking, stir frequently while cooking to separate pasta; you can also add a few drops of oil to the boiling water as it cooks.

❖ Cider or white *vinegar* is used for general cooking unless specified. Distilled white vinegar is usually preferred for pickling or canning, as it is clear and colorless. Wine vinegars and herbed vinegars are usually specified, but may be substituted.

❖ When *salt* is called for use iodized salt unless specified. However, fine sea salt may be substituted. Use kosher salt (coarse, natural sea salt) or rock salt (salt crystals used in freezing ice cream) only when specified.

❖ *Sugar* refers to granulated white sugar unless specified. Brown sugar refers to light brown sugar (dark brown sugar contains more molasses). When brown sugar is given it often specifies "packed," meaning to pack it down to measure. Powdered sugar is also known as confectioners' sugar. Measure without sifting, then sift if specified or if too lumpy.

❖ *Deep-fat frying* refers to foods cooked in at least 2 inches of oil heated before foods are added. Use a food thermometer when a specified temperature is called for. Special deep-frying pans are available which may reduce the amount of spattering and control the temperature, but any sauce pan or skillet can be used. Keep a good distance to avoid spattering and burns while cooking.

❖ *Baking* refers to foods baked in the oven at a temperature generally ranging from 250 to 400 degrees, unless specified. Keep ovens calibrated for accurate temperature control.

❖ *Grilling* refers to foods that are grilled on a barbecue grill over low to hot coals.

❖ *Broiling* refers to cooking foods under the broiler about 2 to 4 inches from the source of heat. Heating under the broiler to brown tops of casserole dishes, such as dishes covered with cheese, bread crumbs or sugar should be in flame– or heat-proof containers. Glass and porcelain break under intense heat and should not be used.

❖ *Searing* refers to food cooked quickly in skillet using some or no fat.

INGREDIENT GUIDE

Achiote–tropical tree whose seeds and powder ground from the seeds, are used in Latin American cooking. Available in Latin grocery stores and many supermarkets.

Annatto powder–a natural reddish yellow coloring from a tropical American tree. Sometimes available at Latin food stores. Yellow food coloring can be substituted.

Arrowroot–flavorless starch from tropical tuber used to thicken sauces and gravies.

Baking soda–sometimes referred to as soda. Use strictly as instructed.

Bread crumbs–usually dry bread crumbs, without seasoning.

Bulgur–known as cracked wheat.

Butter–refers to salted butter, unless specified as unsalted. Margarine may be substituted. Do not use whipped butter or whipped margarine in recipes calling for plain butter or margarine.

Chiles, fresh–chiles vary from mild to very hot and can be found fresh or packaged in Latin grocery stores and supermarkets:
Poblano, Ancho, Pasilla Negra–mild to medium hot, plump and dark for stuffing
California or Anaheim–mild, long, green
Serrano–very small, very hot, green or red
Jalapeño–small, also canned, green

Chinese Chile Oil–oil which has been cooked and seasoned with hot dried chiles. Can be found at any Asian grocery store or many supermarkets.

Chocolate–there are many types used for cooking and candy–making:
Dark Germans chocolate–bitter chocolate sweetened with sugar.
Sweet cooking chocolate bars–a blend of chocolate, sugar and cocoa butter.
Semisweet–blend of chocolate, sugar and cocoa butter; comes in bars or packages of squares.
Semisweet pieces or chips–comes in packages.
White chocolate–milk and sugar blended with cocoa butter
Milk chocolate–made with sugar, milk and vanilla; used as an eating chocolate, but can be melted.
Unsweetened chocolate–bitter chocolate from roasted cocoa beans
Carob–an eastern Mediterranean tree whose pods and seeds when ground into a powder become a substitute for chocolate.
Unsweetened cocoa powder–powdered chocolate with cocoa butter removed.
Instant cocoa or instant chocolate drink mix–blend of cocoa, sugar, milk solids, flavoring used in beverages. Do not use in cooking.
Fine European chocolates–dark, sweet, expensive chocolates such as Valhrona, often used in gourmet chocolate dessert recipes.
Mexican Chocolate–a spiced chocolate that comes in tablets and is used in Mexican beverages and sauces. To substitute, for 1 (3-ounce) Mexican chocolate tablet use 3 ounces semisweet chocolate, 2 tablespoons sugar, $\frac{1}{4}$ teaspoon vanilla and $\frac{1}{2}$ teaspoon cinnamon.

Coconut–
Shredded-dry, sweetened, comes in packages.

Coconut–
  *Fresh, grated–*shredded from fresh coconut
  *Flake–*moist and available in cans or bags.

*Coconut milk–*available in cans, fresh milk can be extracted by blending chunks of coconut with 1 cup fresh coconut water from the coconut. Squeeze through damp cheesecloth or strainer.

*Coconut Cream–*cream of coconut milk that rises to the surface. Available in cans.

*Phyllo Dough–*paper thin sheets of fresh dough used to make pastries in Middle Eastern and Mediterranean cuisines. Also available frozen.

*Fish Sauce–*known as nam pla; fermented fish brine used widely in Thai and other Southeast Asian cuisines.

*Five Spice Powder–*blend of star anise, anise pepper, fennel, cloves and cinnamon, found in any Asian grocery store or market.

*Flour–*Several types of flours are now available in supermarkets and health food stores:
  *All-purpose flour–*used for all baking; milled from hard and soft wheat.
  *Bread flour–*a flour high in gluten content or hard wheat. Available in health food stores and some supermarkets.
  *Cake flour–*a very fine-textured flour milled from soft wheat.
  *Masa Harina–*powdered corn meal treated with lye; used for making corn tortillas; found in Latin markets.
  *Pastry flour–*texture is a cross between cake flour and all-purpose flour, used in pie pastries to make dough flaky and tender.
  *Potato flour–*made from potatoes, this fine granulated flour is used to thicken sauces.
  *Self-rising flour–*enriched, all-purpose flour to which baking powder and salt are added.

*Hoisin–*a Chinese sauce made from soy beans and spices, available in Asian markets.

*Kang Pet Dang–*a red curry paste used in Thai curry dishes, available at Thai food markets.

*Ketjap–*dark, Indonesian soy-based product used as a condiment in Thai cooking. Available in most Asian grocery stores.

*Lemon Grass–*a lemon-scented grassy stalk used to flavor foods in Asian cooking.

*Liquid Smoke–*used to impart smoky, charcoal flavor to cooked foods–also known as Hickory seasoning or charcoal seasoning.

*Mirin–*Japanese sweet rice wine used for cooking.

*Mascarpone–*sometimes referred to as Italian cream cheese, this creamy cheese is used mostly in desserts. Available in gourmet stores and some supermarkets.

*Noodles–*available at Asian markets:
  *Kishimen–*a flat fettuccine type noodle, a variation of Japanese udon used in place of rice in sukiyaki dishes.
  *Ramen–*same as Chinese egg noodles (bon mein), used in soups.
  *Rice Sticks–*also known as rice noodles, mai fun in Chinese or sen mee in Thai cuisine. They are a thin, brittle noodle made from rice flour. When deep-fried, they puff up and become white and crispy. Use in salads and soups.

Soba–thick or thin and caramel-colored from buckwheat flour, these noodles are eaten like udon, hot and wet or cold and slightly dry or on ice for summer salads.

Somen–the thinnest Japanese noodle made from wheat flour and prepared like soba or rice sticks.

Udon–fat, white wheat noodles sold fresh in vacuum packs or dried. A popular Japanese noodle used chiefly in soups.

Sai Fun–called cellophane noodles or bean threads or silver threads are like rice sticks but slightly thinner and more translucent, made from mung bean. They require soaking. Used in soups and stir-fry dishes.

Vermicelli–egg noodles wrapped like folded ribbons or packaged like Italian noodles. Used in soups, such as Pad Thai, and Chinese stir-fry, pan fried chow mein and braised low mein noodle dishes.

Orgeat–a milky, non-alcoholic syrup made from barley and sweetened almonds. Used mainly to flavor tropical drinks such as mai-tai's.

Panko–very fine Japanese bread crumbs used for delicate breading of meat and vegetable dishes. Available at many supermarkets and Japanese grocery stores.

Plum Sauce–a condiment made from plums, apricots, chile and vinegar; used with roasted meats and game. Available in Asian markets.

Preserved grape leaves–can be made by parboiling fresh leaves and storing them in olive oil or salt brine. They are also available in jars at Middle Eastern or gourmet food stores.

Shaoshing wine–Chinese rice wine found in most Asian grocery stores and some supermarkets.

Soy Bean Pudding–comes in several brands, flavors, individual and large sizes, available in health food stores.

Sterilized egg whites–when raw egg whites are called for in recipes that do not require cooking, we suggest using sterilized egg whites found in supermarkets.

Tamari–soy seasoning used in Japanese cooking, particularly for basting broiled or grilled foods.

Tahini–a paste made of sesame seeds; available canned and used as a dressing or spread on meat and vegetable dishes. Available in Middle Eastern grocery stores and many supermarkets.

Tofu–Bland tasting soy bean curd processed in blocks with custard-like consistency.

Vegetable Spray–a blend of vegetable oil, water and preservatives used as a spray on pans to prevent foods from sticking.

Vinegars–

Wine vinegars–may be made with white, red or champagne wines, cider, sherry or rice, and flavored with herbs, such as tarragon, or fruit, such as raspberry vinegar.

Balsamic vinegar–a pungent aged Italian vinegar made from the must of grape juice, used to flavor sauces, dress salads, vegetables and cheeses.

Black Chinkiang vinegar–an Asian soy product vinegar, available in Asian markets.

Wasabi–a paste made from horseradish powder used as a condiment in sushi and sashimi dishes in the Japanese cuisine.

APPETIZERS

There are some unusual appetizer recipes in this chapter that will give you pause. *Texas Caviar* is one such recipe as it is made with black-eyed peas, not caviar. There are old favorites, too, such as California guacamole which almost every Californian prepares for parties. But since we also pride ourselves on our ethnic range, the chapter includes recipes for *Mee Krob*, the Thai popcorn-ish appetizer you can't stop eating, and stuffed grape leaves. Among the latest favorites are recipes for caponata and salmon tartar.

❖

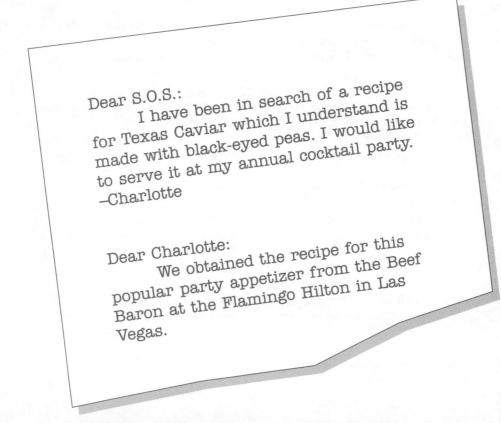

Dear S.O.S.:
    I have been in search of a recipe for Texas Caviar which I understand is made with black-eyed peas. I would like to serve it at my annual cocktail party.
–Charlotte

Dear Charlotte:
    We obtained the recipe for this popular party appetizer from the Beef Baron at the Flamingo Hilton in Las Vegas.

ACAPULCO'S GUACAMOLE

The guacamole served at the Acapulco Mexican restaurants is a good example of the type Californians prefer.

> *3 medium avocados*
> *½ teaspoon salt*
> *⅓ teaspoon finely minced garlic*
> *½ tablespoon finely minced cilantro*
> *1 tomato, peeled, seeded and finely chopped*

Assemble and measure ingredients then mix just before serving. Mash avocados with fork but do not mix into smooth paste. Add salt which has been mashed with garlic. Add cilantro and taste. Add more seasoning, if wanted. Fold tomato into guacamole but do not mix too smoothly. It should be a little chunky. Serve immediately. Makes 6 to 8 servings. Serve as a dip for chips or vegetable crudité and as sauce for pita or tortilla sandwiches.

❖

CARLOS' N' CHARLIE'S TUNA DIP

This is the updated version of an old favorite dip from Carlos' N' Charlie's, a Mexican-style restaurant and celebrity hangout in Hollywood.

> *1 (12 ½-ounce) can tuna, drained*
> *1 ½ to 2 jalapeno chiles, seeded and stemmed*
> *1 (1-inch) piece green onion (green part only)*
> *1 (1-inch) piece celery*
> *¼ to ½ cup mayonnaise*
> *Salt, pepper*
> *3 to 4 leaves cilantro, chopped*

Blend tuna, jalapenos, green onion and celery in food processor or blender (do not purée). Blend in mayonnaise and salt and pepper to taste. Blend to desired consistency. Sprinkle with cilantro. Makes 2 cups.

❖

MATSUHISA SALMON TARTAR

Those who eat raw fish will find this version of tartar outstanding. The recipe is from masters of raw fish cookery, Matsuhisa, a Japanese restaurant in Los Angeles with a popular sushi bar.

3 ounces salmon fillet, finely chopped
1 ounce caviar
1 small garlic clove, minced
1 tablespoon Maui onion, chopped
1 teaspoon minced green onion
Wasabi Sauce

Mix salmon, caviar, garlic, onion and green onion until combined. Serve in mound with Wasabi Sauce on side. Makes 2 appetizer servings.

WASABI SAUCE

1 ounce wasabi powder
⅓ cup water
2 ½ tablespoons soy sauce

Mix wasabi in water. Stir in soy sauce. Makes about ⅓ cup.

❖

BEEF BARON TEXAS CAVIAR

We have printed many recipes for mock caviar (also called cowboy caviar because it uses black-eyed peas) over the years, but this, from the Beef Baron at the Flamingo Hilton in Las Vegas, is the most requested.

½ pound black-eyed peas

1 cup diced green pepper

¼ cup diced pimientos

1 cup diced onion

½ cup finely chopped green onions

2 tablespoons chopped garlic

¼ cup finely chopped jalapeno chiles

1 cup bottled Italian dressing

Salt, pepper

Soak peas in cold water to cover overnight. Drain and rinse. Cover with fresh water and bring to boil. Reduce heat, cover and simmer 1 hour or longer until tender. Do not overcook.

Drain, rinse and place drained peas in large bowl. Add green pepper, pimientos, onion, green onions, garlic, chiles and Italian dressing. Season to taste with salt and pepper. Makes about 4 cups.

❖

PASADENA HILTON'S CAPONATA

Hotel restaurants such as the Pasadena Hilton were quick to adopt the caponata made popular by Italian restaurants. Serve on crusty bread or crackers.

2 large eggplants
Salt
1 large sweet green pepper
1 large sweet red pepper
1 large sweet yellow pepper
1 cup chopped fresh basil
5 ounces finely grated Pecorino Romano cheese
Balsamic Vinaigrette

Peel and slice eggplant. Sprinkle slices with salt and set aside 30 minutes to draw out bitter juices from eggplant. Rinse thoroughly and dry well.

Grill eggplant on char-broiler or under broiler until barely cooked, about 2 minutes on each side. Cool.

Grill green, red and yellow peppers with skin on, until skin is charred and blistered. Place peppers in paper bag and set aside until peppers are cool enough to handle. Peel peppers and remove seeds and stems. Cut peppers and eggplant into ½-inch squares. Toss with basil and cheese. Add Balsamic Vinaigrette. Marinate at least 3 hours. Makes 12 appetizer servings.

BALSAMIC VINAIGRETTE

½ cup balsamic vinegar
¼ cup extra-virgin olive oil
1 tablespoon minced garlic
2 teaspoons sugar
1 teaspoon freshly ground black pepper
2 teaspoons salt

Combine balsamic vinegar, olive oil, garlic, sugar, pepper and salt. Mix well. Makes about ¾ cup.

❖

EGGPLANT CAVIAR

Eggplant caviar is used as a dip or topping for pita bread sandwishes.

2 medium eggplants
1 cup water
1 cup drained canned tomatoes, crushed
1 tablespoon tomato paste
1 clove garlic, crushed 1 teaspoon
1 teaspoon lemon juice
1 teaspoon vinegar
¼ cup olive oil
1 tablespoon capers
few drops hot pepper sauce
1 tablespoon minced onion
1 teaspoon sugar

Peel and slice eggplants. Cook in 1 cup water until tender. Drain and mash. Add tomatoes, tomato paste, garlic, lemon juice, vinegar, oil, capers, hot sauce, onion and sugar. Chill several hours or overnight. Serve as spread for bread or crackers. Makes 2⅓ cups.

❖

BRUSCHETTA

Modern Italian chefs introduced Californians to the myriad versions of bruschetta.

12 (2-inch round) slices French or Italian bread
Olive oil
4 Italian plum tomatoes, diced
Balsamic vinegar to taste
Salt, pepper
1 tablespoon minced fresh basil

Placed bread slices on baking sheet. Drizzle lightly with oil. Toast on both sides under broiler. Set aside. Place tomatoes in bowl. Sprinkle with balsamic vinegar, and salt and pepper to taste. Spoon onto toasted bread slices. Sprinkle lightly with basil. Makes 12 canapés.

SIMPLIFIED MEE KROB

Mee Krob (or Mee Grob), means noodle in Siamese. The dish comes in varying degrees of sweetness and complexity. Here is a moderately sweet, simplified version from Chan Dara, a Thai restaurant in Hollywood.

2 green onions
½ small carrot
½ cup sugar
½ cup white vinegar
¼ teaspoon salt
Oil for deep frying
6 ounces boneless chicken, cut into strips
¼ pound deveined, peeled shrimp
2 eggs, beaten
4 ounces rice noodles

Cut green onions diagonally into 1½- to 2-inch slices. Cut carrot diagonally into long, thin slices, then cut carrot slices into shreds. Set green onions and carrot aside for garnish.

Combine sugar, vinegar and salt in small saucepan. Bring to boil and boil vigorously until slightly thickened and resembles syrup. Set aside.

Heat oil for deep frying in large skillet. Add chicken and fry until almost done. Add shrimp and fry with chicken until pink. Drain chicken and shrimp on paper towels. Add eggs to skillet and cook until browned and crisp, stirring constantly. Drain.

Fry rice noodles in skillet in 2 or 3 batches until puffed and lightly browned, turning once. Drain on paper towels.

Heat wok. Add syrup and bring to boil. Add shrimp and chicken, mix with syrup and cook until liquid evaporates out of chicken and shrimp. (Mixture must be dry so noodles will not be soggy.) Add noodles and stir rapidly. Add some egg, leaving a little for garnish. Stir to mix. When noodles are well mixed and pan is dry, turn out onto serving platter. Top with green onions, shredded carrot and reserved egg. Makes 8 servings.

❖

Stuffed Grape Leaves *(Dolmas)*

Readers introduced to Middle Eastern cuisine found these meat and rice-stuffed grape leaf appetizers known as "dolmas" intriguing.

2 large onions, chopped
½ cup oil
¾ cup rice
1 ½ pounds ground lamb or beef
1 tablespoon fresh minced or 1 teaspoon dried mint
Salt, pepper
⅛ teaspoon ground cinnamon
¼ cup pine nuts
Preserved grape leaves

Cook onion in oil until tender, but not browned. Add rice and cook, stirring, until pale golden. Remove from heat and combine with meat, mint, salt and pepper to taste, cinnamon and nuts. Mix thoroughly.

Spread grape leaves flat and place spoonful of meat mixture in center of each. Roll up into finger shapes, tucking in ends. Place rolls close together, seam sides down, in casserole. Add water to cover and simmer 40 to 45 minutes until rice is tender. Add more water to keep rolls covered at all times. Drain off water before serving. Makes 12 appetizer servings.

SOUPS

Readers love soups and these are our most frequently requested recipes. They are diverse in character and style and they range from a spicy tomato soup, to an elegant roasted eggplant and sweet red pepper soup by a contemporary chef. Many are recipes that readers have tried and enjoyed at restaurants, such as a grain and vegetable soup from a health food restaurant, and cucumber soup from the Velvet Turtle chain in California.

❖

Dear S.O.S.:
    I would love to have the recipe for the tomato soup served at Kokomo's Steak House at the Mirage Hotel in Las Vegas.
–Tori

Dear Tori:
    This soup gets into the spirit of things with a splash of gin for flavor.

Velvet Turtle Cucumber Soup

The Velvet Turtle chain of restaurants serve this outstanding creamy cucumber soup that readers clamor for year in and year out.

1 onion, coarsely chopped

1 cup chopped leek (white part only)

1 large cucumber, peeled, seeded and diced

Butter or margarine

Salt, pepper

2 tablespoons dry white wine

2 cups water

1 ½ teaspoons chicken base

2 tablespoons flour

½ cup whipping cream

½ teaspoon lemon juice

5 drops hot pepper sauce

Dash chopped fresh or dried dill

½ cup half and half, if needed

Sour cream, optional

Lemon wedges, parsley

Sauté onion, leek and cucumber, reserving ½ cup diced cucumber, in 2 tablespoons butter until onion is transparent. Season to taste with salt and pepper. Cook and stir until blended. Add wine, water and chicken base and bring to boil. Melt 2 tablespoons butter in small pan and blend in flour. Add to onion mixture and simmer 1 hour.

Process soup in blender, about 15 seconds, then strain through fine sieve. Add whipping cream, lemon juice, pepper sauce, dill and reserved diced cucumber. Cool soup completely, correct seasoning and add half and half if soup is too thick. Serve in chilled soup cups. Add ½ teaspoon sour cream to each and garnish with lemon wedge and parsley, if desired. Makes 6 servings.

❖

KOKOMO'S GIN TOMATO SOUP

Kokomo's Steak House at the Mirage Hotel in Las Vegas pleased our readers by sharing this soup recipe with its Bloody Mary flavors.

2 tablespoons butter
½ cup finely diced onion
2 cloves garlic, crushed
20 Roma tomatoes, peeled, seeded and diced
2 cups tomato juice
½ teaspoon chopped fresh thyme
½ teaspoon chopped fresh rosemary
½ teaspoon chopped fresh basil
Dash sugar
Salt, pepper
16 strips bacon, cut into fine julienne
20 mushrooms, cut into fine julienne
¼ cup gin
½ cup whipping cream or half and half
½ cup chicken stock

Melt butter in soup pan over medium heat. Add onion and garlic and sauté until tender. Add tomatoes, tomato juice, thyme, rosemary and basil. Cover and simmer 25 minutes, adding more liquid if necessary for desired consistency. Add sugar and season to taste with salt and pepper.

Sauté bacon and mushrooms strips in skillet. Drain off excess fat. Add gin and carefully ignite. When flames die down add tomato soup mixture, whipping cream and chicken stock. Bring quickly to boil. Adjust seasonings to taste. Serve at once. Makes 8 servings.

❖

MANHATTAN CLAM CHOWDER

Manhattan Clam Chowder is the request of readers who enjoy clam chowder made with tomatoes instead of milk and cream. This is from the Odyessy Restaurant in Granada Hills, California.

> *1 cup chopped onion*
>
> *1 cup chopped celery*
>
> *½ cup diced green pepper*
>
> *2 tablespoons butter or margarine*
>
> *2 (10-ounce) cans clams, undrained*
>
> *Bottled clam juice*
>
> *1 bay leaf*
>
> *Dash dried thyme*
>
> *Dash dried oregano*
>
> *Salt, pepper*
>
> *½ cup tomato paste*
>
> *1 cup diced tomatoes*
>
> *1 tablespoon cornstarch*

Sauté onion, celery and green pepper in butter until tender. Drain liquor from canned clams and combine with clam juice to make 1 quart.

Add clams and juice, bay leaf, thyme and oregano to sautéed vegetables and season to taste with salt and pepper. Cover and simmer 1 hour.

Stir in tomato paste and tomatoes. Simmer 5 minutes or longer. Mix cornstarch with small amount of water to make thin paste and add to soup for thickening. Simmer until soup is slightly thickened. Makes 2 quarts.

❖

ART RYON'S WHITE CLAM CHOWDER

The late Art Ryon, who wrote a restaurant review column in the Los Angeles Times in the fifties and sixties, shared his simple, to-the-point recipe with readers. It's sometimes known as New England Clam Chowder.

6 to 8 slices bacon, cut into $\frac{1}{4}$-inch strips

3 large white onions, cut into quarters

4 potatoes, peeled and diced

1 (6 $\frac{1}{2}$-ounce) can minced clams

1 (7-ounce) can chopped clams

2 quarts milk, about

Worcestershire sauce

Butter or margarine

Salt, pepper

Finely chopped parsley

Sauté bacon in large soup pot until crisp. Add onions and sauté until lightly browned. Stir in potatoes, undrained clams and milk. Add Worcestershire and butter to taste. Season to taste with salt and pepper. Cook, uncovered, over low heat (do not boil) until potatoes are tender, abut 30 minutes. Sprinkle with parsley. Makes 4 to 6 servings.

❖

Moroccan Lentil Soup *(Harira)*

Harira, the national soup of Morocco, eaten there for breakfast, lunch and dinner, has had a great welcome among readers who have learned about its hearty attributes.

½ pound lamb stew meat, diced

8 cups beef broth or water

1 large carrot, sliced diagonally

Salt, pepper

4 ripe tomatoes, peeled and crushed

1 cup lentils, rinsed

½ teaspoon saffron threads

1 large onion, quartered

1 cup chopped cilantro

1 cup chopped parsley

Juice of 1 lemon

2 tablespoons butter

2 tablespoons flour

Lemon wedges

Place lamb in large saucepan with broth, carrot and salt and pepper to taste. Bring to boil, reduce heat and cover. Simmer over low heat 1 hour, or until meat is almost done.

Add tomatoes, lentils, saffron and onion. Simmer, covered, over low heat 40 minutes or until lentils are cooked. Add cilantro, ½ cup parsley and lemon juice.

Melt butter in small saucepan and stir in flour until smooth. Stir gradually into soup. Stir over medium heat until soup is slightly thickened, about 5 minutes. Sprinkle with remaining ½ cup parsley. Serve with lemon wedges. Makes 6 to 8 servings.

❖

HAPPY HOLIDAYS PUMPKIN SOUP

This basic pumpkin soup recipe from our old files is spiked with sherry in the spirit of a festive holiday meal.

2 tablespoons butter or margarine

1 small green pepper, diced

2 tomatoes, peeled and chopped

1 small onion, chopped

2 sprigs parsley

¼ teaspoon crumbled dry thyme

1 bay leaf

2 cups mashed cooked or canned pumpkin

2 cups chicken broth

1 tablespoon flour

½ cup half and half

½ teaspoon ground nutmeg

½ teaspoon sugar

Salt

2 tablespoons dry sherry, optional

Melt butter in large kettle. Add green pepper, tomatoes, onion, parsley, thyme and bay leaf and sauté about 5 minutes. Add pumpkin and chicken broth. Simmer 20 minutes. Strain and return to pan. Blend flour with half and half and stir into strained soup. Add nutmeg and sugar and season to taste with salt. Heat, stirring often, and bring slowly to boil. Add sherry. Simmer 3 minutes. Serve hot. Makes 4 to 6 servings.

❖

Xiomara's Roasted Eggplant and Red Pepper Soup

Chef Patrick Healy, of Xiomara in Pasadena, California, created this soup. It has only a little more than 100 calories per serving and was selected as one of the Los Angeles Times 10 best recipes for 1990.

3 large Japanese eggplants
Salt, pepper
Extra-virgin olive oil
2 sweet red peppers
1 large onion, sliced
4 cloves garlic, crushed
1 quart chicken stock
1 bunch fresh basil

Wash eggplants and split lengthwise in halves. Lightly season with salt and pepper and sprinkle with olive oil to taste.

Roast eggplants at 400 degrees 45 minutes or until tender and golden brown. Purée flesh with skin in blender or food processor. Set aside.

Place peppers under broiler until skins are scorched on all sides. Place in plastic food bag 10 minutes to soften, then peel and remove seeds and stems. Purée flesh in food processor until smooth. Set aside.

Heat 1 tablespoon olive oil in skillet. Add onion and garlic and sauté until tender. Cover to sweat over very low heat 5 minutes. Add roasted eggplant pureé and chicken stock to onion-garlic mixture.

Cook over low heat 15 minutes until flavors blend and mixture is heated through. Purée mixture in blender or food processor until smooth, then strain into clean bowl. Season to taste with salt and pepper.

Cut basil leaves into tiny cubes, resembling confetti.

Place each serving of soup in deep bowl. Spoon sweet red pepper purée in center and swirl into soup. Drizzle lightly with olive oil, if desired. Sprinkle with basil. Makes 6 servings.

❖

SALAMAGUNDI'S SOPA DE TORTILLA

The Salamagundi restaurant chain on the West Coast helped popularize this Mexican soup topped with tortilla chips and cheese, then broiled to melt the cheese.

1 (3-pound) chicken, cut up
4 quarts water
1 teaspoon celery seeds
1 teaspoon black peppercorns
2 whole cloves garlic
1 (1-pound) can whole peeled tomatoes, broken up
1 green pepper, cut into 1-inch cubes
1 onion, cut into 1-inch cubes
3 sprigs cilantro
1 clove garlic, minced
½ teaspoon ground cumin
¼ teaspoon cayenne pepper
¼ teaspoon white pepper
1 (10-ounce) package frozen cut corn
4 green onions, diced
Salt
1 cup cooked rice
4 sprigs parsley, minced
Tortilla chips
Shredded Cheddar cheese

Place chicken, water, celery seeds, peppercorns and whole garlic cloves in large heavy saucepan. Bring to boil. Cover and simmer 35 to 45 minutes or until chicken is tender. Remove chicken from broth, cool, bone and cut meat into 1-inch pieces. Set aside.

Strain broth and return to pot. Add tomatoes, green pepper, onion, cilantro, garlic, cumin, cayenne and white pepper. Bring to boil. Reduce heat, cover and simmer 30 minutes. Add corn and green onions. Cook 10 minutes. Season to taste with salt.

Stir in reserved chicken, rice and parsley. To serve, spoon soup into flame-proof tureen. Top with tortilla chips, then cheese. Place under broiler just until cheese melts. Makes 6 to 8 servings.

❖

Follow Your Heart Creamy Winter Grains Soup

Health concerns about heart disease are probably responsible for the creation of this hearty soup from Follow Your Heart restaurant in Canoga Park, California.

½ cup whole-wheat berries
Water
⅔ cup lentils
¼ cup barley
½ cup short grain brown rice
¼ cup raw, lightly salted butter
2 teaspoons dried thyme leaves
1 ½ cups cubed red or russet potatoes
1 ½ cups sliced carrots
1 ½ cups sliced celery
1 ½ cups diced yellow onions
1 teaspoon ground celery seeds
2 large cloves garlic, pressed
1 tablespoon vegetable seasoned salt
1 tablespoon salt-free vegetable powder
1 tablespoon onion powder
1 tablespoon granulated garlic
¼ cup dried parsley flakes
¼ cup soy sauce
1 cup fresh or frozen corn kernels
1 cup fresh or frozen peas
1 (3-ounce) package cream cheese
1 cup sour cream
1 cup shredded sharp Cheddar cheese
Red pepper
Parsley sprigs

Soak wheat berries in 2 cups water. In heavy 6-quart pot, combine soaked wheat with liquid, 8 cups water, lentils, barley, brown rice, butter and thyme. Bring to boil, reduce heat, cover and simmer over medium heat 20 minutes.

Add potatoes, carrots, celery, onions, celery seeds and garlic. Bring again to simmer and continue to cook, covered, until vegetables and grains are tender, about 30 minutes, stirring occasionally. Add vegetable seasoned salt, vegetable powder, onion powder, granulated garlic, parsley flakes, soy sauce, corn and peas. Reduce heat.

Follow Your Heart Creamy Winter Grains Soup (continued)

Blend ½ cup water, cream cheese, sour cream and Cheddar cheese and add to soup. Season to taste with red pepper and serve garnished with parsley. Makes 8 to 10 generous servings.

Note: Vegetable seasoned salt and salt-free vegetable powder are available in most natural-food stores.

❖

TWO MELON SOUP

Tasters at the Los Angeles Times kitchen loved the two-toned effect of this delightful chilled soup.

> *1 ripe cantaloupe, peeled, seeded and coarsely chopped*
>
> *2 tablespoons lemon juice or to taste*
>
> *½ ripe honeydew melon, peeled, seeded and coarsely chopped*
>
> *3 tablespoons lime juice or to taste*
>
> *1 ½ teaspoons minced mint leaves or to taste*
>
> *Sour cream, optional*
>
> *Additional mint sprigs for garnish*

In food processor or blender, combine cantaloupe and lemon juice and process in batches until smooth. Chill in covered bowl at least 3 hours or overnight.

In food processor or blender, process honeydew melon, lime juice and mint leaves in batches until very smooth. Chill in covered bowl at least 3 hours or overnight. Do not combine melon mixtures.

Using 2 measuring cups containing each melon soup, pour equal amounts of soups at same time into individual chilled bowls. Garnish with sour cream if desired, and sprig of mint. Makes about 7 cups.

BREADS

Those who love to bake will enjoy the variety of breads in this chapter. Those who are discovering the joys of baking for the first time will find the recipes user-friendly. We have broadly classified bread to cover all bread products, including muffins, French toast, pancakes, pretzels and sticky buns. When working with bread recipes, stick to the recipe. Chemical balance of ingredients relies on strict formulation and any tampering might alter the results. When in doubt, grease pans unless specified. Use conventional shortening or vegetable sprays. For best results measure with standard measuring cups and spoons, using level measures. Gather and measure ingredients ahead of time for ease and efficiency.

❖

Dear S.O.S.:
    I've been a big fan of Bullock's department store tea room popovers. Do you have a recipe?
–Doreen

Dear Doreen:
    Sure do. A traditional deep-pocket iron popover pan works best to help "pop" these gargantuan popovers.

ONION LOVERS' TWIST

Onion lovers love this twist filled with garlicky onion and cheese.

1 package dry yeast
$\frac{1}{4}$ cup warm water
4 cups flour
$\frac{1}{4}$ cup sugar
1 $\frac{1}{2}$ teaspoons salt
$\frac{1}{2}$ cup hot water
$\frac{1}{2}$ cup milk
$\frac{1}{4}$ cup butter or margarine, softened
1 egg
Onion Filling

In large mixer bowl, dissolve yeast in warm water. Add 2 cups flour, sugar, salt, hot water, milk, butter and egg. Blend at low speed until moistened. Beat 2 minutes at medium speed. Stir in remaining flour by hand to form soft dough. Cover and let rise in warm place until light and doubled in size, 45 to 60 minutes. Punch down dough. Toss on floured surface until no longer sticky. Roll dough to 18x12-inch rectangle and spread with Onion Filling. Cut lengthwise into 3 (18x4-inch) strips. Starting with 18-inch side, roll up each strip, seal edges and ends. On baking sheet, braid 3 rolls together. Cover and let rise in warm place until light and doubled in size, 45 to 60 minutes. Bake at 350 degrees 30 to 35 minutes or until golden brown. Serve warm or cold. Makes 1 large loaf.

Note: To make 2 small loaves, cut 3 filled rolls in half crosswise before braiding. Braid each set of rolls separately on greased baking sheet and bake as directed.

ONION FILLING

$\frac{1}{4}$ cup butter or margarine
1 cup minced onion or $\frac{1}{4}$ cup instant minced onion
1 tablespoon grated Parmesan cheese
1 tablespoon sesame or poppy seeds
1 teaspoon garlic salt
1 teaspoon paprika

Melt butter in saucepan, add onion, cheese, sesame seeds, garlic salt and paprika and mix well.

MAHALIA JACKSON'S MONKEY BREAD

The late Mahalia Jackson, the gospel singer, shared her recipe for Monkey Bread, a buttery pull-apart bread that can be made in roomy molds such as springform, angel food or Bundt pans.

1 quart milk
¼ cup sugar
4 teaspoons salt
2 tablespoons chilled shortening
1 package dry or cake yeast
¼ cup lukewarm water
12 cups flour, about
Melted shortening
1 pound butter or margarine

Scald milk in saucepan. Add sugar, salt and shortening. Cool mixture to lukewarm.

Sprinkle or crumble yeast in bowl with lukewarm water and stir until dissolved.

Stir dissolved yeast into lukewarm milk mixture. Gradually add flour to milk mixture, mixing well. Add enough flour to make dough stiff enough to be handled easily.

Turn dough onto floured surface and knead until smooth and satiny. Shape dough into 4 loaves. Brush surface lightly with melted shortening. Cover and let rise in warm place free from drafts until doubled in bulk. Melt butter, then cut each loaf into thick slices and dip slices in butter. Place slices in roomy molds with room to expand. Let rise again. Bake at 400 degrees 40 minutes or until golden and crusty. Let cool before slicing. Makes 4 loaves, about 32 slices.

❖

SAN FRANCISCO SOURDOUGH FRENCH BREAD

Here's a San Francisco-style sourdough French bread with a recipe for the sourdough starter which should get you off to a good beginning.

> *1 package dry yeast*
> *1 cup warm water*
> *2 tablespoons sugar*
> *1 ½ cups Sourdough Starter*
> *5 cups flour, about*
> *2 teaspoons salt*
> *Rice flour or cornmeal*

Sprinkle yeast over warm water in large bowl. Let soften 5 minutes. Stir in sugar and Sourdough Starter, then gradually add 4 cups flour mixed with salt. Cover with damp towel and let rise in warm place 1½ hours.

Turn dough onto floured board and work in about 1 cup flour or enough so dough is no longer sticky. Knead until satiny, about 5 minutes.

Shape dough into one large round or 2 oval loaves. Set loaves on baking sheet and sprinkle with rice flour or cornmeal. Let rise again in warm place 1½ hours. Place shallow pan of water on lower shelf of oven heated to 400 degrees. Using sharp knife, make diagonal slashes in bread. Bake at 400 degrees 40 to 50 minutes until crust is medium dark brown in color.

SOURDOUGH STARTER

> *1 package dry yeast*
> *2 cups warm water*
> *2 cups flour*

Mix yeast, warm water and flour in 1½-quart glass or earthenware container. Cover with cheesecloth. Let stand at room temperature 48 hours. Stir 2 or 3 times. Mixture will ferment, bubble and acquire slightly sour smell. Makes 3 cups.

To use, stir, then pour off as much as recipe requires. Add equal parts flour and water to remaining starter in pot. Stir and let stand a few hours until it bubbles again before covering and refrigerating. Keep replenishing starter with flour and water as necessary.

❖

SQUAW BREAD

Our search for an authentic Squaw bread similar to that sold in bakeries and restaurants throughout California ended happily when Marilyn Martell, a Los Angeles school teacher, and frequent country fair blue-ribbon winner, sent us a recipe she developed.

2 cups water
⅓ cup oil
¼ cup honey
¼ cup raisins
5 tablespoons brown sugar, packed
2 packages dry yeast
¼ cup warm water
2 ½ cup unbleached all-purpose flour, about
3 cups whole-wheat flour
1 ½ cups rye flour
½ cup instant nonfat milk powder
2 ½ teaspoons salt
Cornmeal
Melted butter

Combine water, oil, honey, raisins and 4 tablespoons brown sugar in blender container. Blend to liquefy.

Soften yeast in warm water with remaining 1 tablespoon brown sugar. Sift together 1 cup unbleached flour, 2 cups whole wheat flour, 1 cup rye flour, nonfat milk powder and salt in large bowl. Add honey mixture and yeast. Beat with mixer at medium speed until smooth, about 2 minutes. Gradually stir in enough of remaining flours to make soft dough that leaves side of bowl. Turn out onto floured surface and knead until smooth and satiny, about 10 to 12 minutes.

Place dough in lightly greased bowl and turn to grease other side. Cover and let rise until doubled, about 1½ hours. Punch dough down and let stand 10 minutes. Shape into 4 round loaves.

Place 2 loaves on each of 2 lightly greased baking sheets sprinkled with cornmeal. Cover and let rise in warm place until light and doubled in size, about 1 hour. Bake at 375 degrees 30 to 35 minutes. Cool on racks. While still hot, brush with melted butter. Makes 4 loaves, each with 8 slices.

❖

JALAPEÑO CORN BREAD

Most readers of *Dear S.O.S.* know and love this Mexican-style corn bread filled with chiles and cheese used for home and party meals.

1 cup cornmeal

1 teaspoon salt

½ teaspoon baking soda

1 (8 ¾-ounce) can cream-style corn

1 cup milk

½ cup oil

1 large onion, chopped

5 canned pickled jalapeno chiles, chopped

2 cups shredded Cheddar cheese

2 eggs, beaten

Combine cornmeal, salt and baking soda. Stir in corn, milk and oil. Add onion, chiles, cheese and eggs and mix.

Turn into greased 9-inch square baking pan. Bake at 350 degrees until set, about 1 hour. Let stand 10 minutes. Cut into squares to serve. Makes 9 servings.

❖

SMOKE HOUSE GARLIC BREAD

The Smoke House restaurant in Burbank claims to have the "world's best garlic bread." Must be. Readers have been clamoring for the recipe for years and still do.

½ cup butter or margarine

2 cloves garlic, ground

1 (1-pound) loaf French bread, cut into 15 slices

2 cups shredded processed American cheese

Melt butter, add garlic and let mixture stand several hours or overnight to blend flavors. Strain off garlic. Brush bread slices with butter mixture, then sprinkle with cheese. Place under broiler until heated and golden brown. Makes 15 slices.

❖

KNOTT'S BERRY FARM CRANBERRY BREAD

Knott's Berry Farm amusement park in Buena Park, California, has supplied us with some of our best bread recipes.

2 cups sifted flour
1 cup sugar
1 1/2 teaspoons baking powder
1 teaspoon salt
1/2 teaspoon baking soda
1/4 cup shortening
3/4 cup orange juice
1 egg, well beaten
1 cup fresh cranberries, chopped coarsely
1/2 cup chopped nuts

Sift flour, sugar, baking powder, salt and baking soda together. Using two knives or pastry blender, cut in shortening. Combine orange juice and egg. Add to dry ingredients, mixing just enough to moisten. Fold in cranberries and nuts. Bake in well-greased 9 x 5-inch pan at 350 degrees 1 hour. Makes 1 loaf.

❖

PERSIMMON BREAD

A bread that brings warmth to the holiday season.

2 cups flour, sifted
2 teaspoons ground cinnamon
2 teaspoons baking soda
1/2 teaspoon salt
1 1/4 cups sugar
1/2 cup raisins
1/2 cup chopped nuts
2 eggs
3/4 cup oil
2 cups puréed ripe persimmon pulp
1 teaspoon lemon juice

Persimmon Bread (continued)

Combine flour, cinnamon, baking soda, salt and sugar. Stir in raisins and nuts. Set aside.

Beat eggs with oil. Add persimmon pulp and lemon juice. Add flour mixture. Mix until just blended.

Turn into 2 greased 8 x 4-inch loaf pans and bake at 350 degrees (325 degrees for glass pans) 1 hour or until wood pick inserted in center comes out clean. Makes 2 loaves, 8 servings each.

Note: Bread will not have high volume.

❖

FRESH STRAWBERRY BREAD

An abundance of fresh strawberries in the garden or market usually prompts requests for this fine bread which freezes well and makes delicious toast.

½ cup butter or margarine
1 cup sugar
½ teaspoon almond extract, or less
2 eggs, separated
2 cups flour
1 teaspoon baking powder
1 teaspoon baking soda
1 teaspoon salt
1 cup crushed or chopped fresh strawberries

Cream together butter, sugar and almond extract. Beat in egg yolks, one at a time. Sift together flour, baking powder, baking soda and salt. Add flour mixture alternately with strawberries to creamed mixture.

Beat egg whites until stiff. Fold into strawberry mixture. Line 9x5-inch loaf pan with greased wax paper. Turn batter into pan. Bake at 350 degrees 50 to 60 minutes or until bread tests done. Cool 15 minutes on rack. Remove from pan and cool. Makes 1 loaf.

❖

MACADAMIA NUT BREAD

When readers discover this Hawaiian bread while visiting the Islands, they invariably request the recipe. We've printed it dozens of times over the years.

3 cups whole macadamia nuts
1 (15 ¼-ounce) can pineapple chunks, very well drained
1 (3 ½-ounce) can flaked coconut
¾ cup sifted flour
¾ cup sugar
½ teaspoon baking powder
½ teaspoon salt
3 eggs
1 teaspoon vanilla

Place nuts, pineapple and coconut in large bowl. Combine flour, sugar, baking powder and salt in sifter and sift over nut mixture. Mix until nuts and fruit are completely coated with flour.

Beat eggs until foamy, then add vanilla. Stir in nut mixture. Spoon into greased, wax paper-lined 8 x 4-inch loaf pan. Bake at 300 degrees 50 minutes or until bread tests done with wood pick. Remove from pan and cool completely. When cool, wrap in foil or plastic wrap and refrigerate. Makes 1 loaf.

❖

RANCHO BERNARDO INN'S WALNUT BREAD

The recipe for a rich walnut bread from Rancho Bernardo Inn in San Diego has been a Christmas favorite for many years.

1 cup butter or margarine
2 cups sugar
4 eggs
4 cups flour
½ teaspoon salt
2 teaspoons baking soda
1 ½ cups chopped walnuts
2 teaspoons vanilla
2 cups sour cream

Rancho Bernardo Inn's Walnut Bread (continued)

Cream butter and sugar until fully blended. Slowly beat in eggs. Sift flour, salt and baking soda and add to egg mixture. Blend in nuts, vanilla and sour cream.

Pour batter into 2 greased and floured 9 x 5-inch loaf pans. Bake at 350 degrees 45 minutes to 1 hour. Cool in pans 10 minutes, then invert onto wire rack. Makes 2 loaves.

❖

CLIFF HOUSE ZUCCHINI BREAD

Home crops of zucchini often prompt requests for this bread recipe from the Cliff House in Playa del Rey, California

3 eggs

2 cups sugar

2 teaspoons vanilla

1 cup oil

3 cups peeled and grated zucchini, drained

3 cups flour

1 teaspoon baking powder

1 teaspoon baking soda

½ teaspoon salt

½ cup raisins, optional

1 cup pecans

1 cup drained crushed pineapple

Beat together eggs, sugar, vanilla and oil in large bowl. Stir in zucchini.

In separate bowl, combine flour, baking powder, baking soda, salt, raisins and pecans. Add to zucchini mixture. Add pineapple and mix well. Pour into greased and floured 9 x 5-inch loaf pan. Bake at 350 degrees 55 to 60 minutes or until wood pick inserted in center comes out clean. Makes 1 loaf, or approximately 8 servings.

❖

OZARK PUMPKIN BREAD

A holiday favorite for as many years as *Dear S.O.S.* has existed.

1 ⅔ cups sifted flour
¼ teaspoon baking powder
1 teaspoon baking soda
⅛ teaspoon salt
½ teaspoon ground cinnamon
½ teaspoon ground nutmeg
⅓ cup shortening
1 ⅓ cups sugar
½ teaspoon vanilla
2 eggs
1 cup mashed cooked or canned pumpkin
⅓ cup sherry
½ cup chopped nuts

Sift flour with baking powder, baking soda, salt, cinnamon and nutmeg. Cream shortening with sugar and vanilla. Add eggs, one at a time, beating well after each addition. Stir in pumpkin. Add flour mixture alternately with sherry and blend well. Stir in nuts.

Turn into well-greased 9 x 5-inch loaf pan and bake at 350 degrees 1 hour or until cake tester inserted in center comes out clean. Turn out onto wire rack to cool. Wrap and refrigerate until ready to slice. Makes 1 loaf.

❖

TAHITIAN LANAI BANANA MUFFINS

Breads, cakes, pies and muffins like this banana muffin recipe, from the Tahitian Lanai in Honolulu, have been a great hit with readers over the years.

1 ½ cups butter or margarine
2 cups sugar
6 eggs, beaten
1 cup mashed bananas
¼ teaspoon vanilla
¼ teaspoon banana flavoring
4 cups cake flour
1 ½ teaspoons baking soda
¼ teaspoon salt

Cream together butter and sugar until light. Add beaten eggs, mashed bananas, vanilla and banana flavoring. Mix well. Sift together flour, baking soda and salt 3 times. Stir into banana mixture. Do not overmix. Spoon into 4 dozen greased muffin cups and bake at 350 degrees 20 minutes, or until golden brown. Makes 4 dozen.

❖

ZUCCHINI MUFFINS

This recipe from former pastry chef Lori Swartz at Chez Melange in Redondo Beach, California, can be baked in a nine-inch cake pan and cut into bars.

3 cups grated zucchini
1 ½ cups oil
3 cups flour
3 cups sugar
4 eggs
½ teaspoon salt
1 ½ teaspoons baking powder
1 teaspoon baking soda
1 ½ teaspoons ground cinnamon
1 teaspoon ground allspice
½ teaspoon ground nutmeg
1 cup chopped nuts

Combine zucchini and oil in large bowl. Add flour, sugar, eggs, salt, baking powder, baking soda, cinnamon, allspice, nutmeg and nuts. Mix until just blended.

Turn into 30 well-greased or paper-lined muffin cups. Bake at 350 degrees 45 minutes or until wood pick inserted in center comes out clean. Makes 30 muffins.

❖

GRISWOLD'S BRAN MUFFINS

Nothing can be more nutritious than these bran muffins from Griswold's bakery and restaurant in Claremont, California. They're loaded with bran cereal, raisins and pineapple.

¼ cup butter or margarine

6 tablespoons brown sugar, packed

1 cup granulated sugar

6 tablespoons honey

1 tablespoon water

½ cup whole-wheat flour

½ cup plus 2 tablespoons cake flour

1 teaspoon salt

½ teaspoon baking soda

½ teaspoon ground cinnamon

½ cup raisins

2 eggs, lightly beaten

¼ cup oil

¼ cup well-drained crushed pineapple

3 cups whole bran cereal

1 ½ cups buttermilk

Cream butter until fluffy and gradually beat in brown sugar and 6 tablespoons granulated sugar. Blend in 2 tablespoons honey and water and whip until fluffy.

Coat 18 to 20 large muffin cups liberally and evenly with mixture. Combine whole-wheat flour and cake flour, remaining 10 tablespoons granulated sugar, salt, baking soda and cinnamon.

Stir in raisins. Add eggs, remaining ¼ cup honey, oil and pineapple and blend. Stir in bran and buttermilk and mix until batter is just blended.

Fill coated muffin pans ¾ full. Bake at 400 degrees 18 to 20 minutes. Remove muffins from pans immediately by turning upside down on racks. Makes 18 to 20 muffins.

CITY SCHOOL SWEET ROLLS

Requests have been coming in for these rolls since the fifties when city school cafeterias served them. Many still do.

4 cakes yeast
2 cups lukewarm milk
½ cup sugar
2 teaspoons salt
½ cup shortening
1 egg
1 cup cake flour
5 cups bread flour
¾ to 1 ½ teaspoons ground nutmeg
¼ cup butter or margarine, melted
Cake Crumb Filling
Powdered Sugar Glaze

Dissolve yeast cakes in lukewarm milk. Combine sugar, salt, shortening and egg in mixing bowl and mix 1 minute at low speed. Add milk mixture and mix 1 minute. Add cake and bread flours and nutmeg and mix only enough for flour to be incorporated, not more than 5 minutes.

Roll out to 18 x 12-inch rectangle. Brush with butter and sprinkle with Cake Crumb Filling. Starting from 18-inch side, roll up jellyroll fashion. Slice into 1-inch slices. Place on greased baking sheets, cut-side down, and pat out fairly flat. Let rise until doubled. Bake at 400 degrees 15 minutes. When partially cooled, brush with Powdered Sugar Glaze. Makes 18 rolls.

CAKE CRUMB FILLING
1 cup plain cake crumbs
½ cup brown sugar, packed
1 teaspoon ground cinnamon

Combine cake crumbs, brown sugar and cinnamon in small bowl and mix well.

POWDERED SUGAR GLAZE
2 cups powdered sugar
¼ cup hot water
1 teaspoon vanilla

Mix powdered sugar with hot water until smooth. Stir in vanilla.

CURRANT SCONES

Scone recipes are easy and quick enough to put together for a last minute brunch or tea.

> *4 cups flour*
> *2 teaspoons baking powder*
> *⅓ cup sugar*
> *½ teaspoon salt*
> *½ cup butter, sliced*
> *½ cup currants*
> *3 eggs*
> *¾ cup whipping cream*

Combine flour, baking powder, sugar and salt in bowl. Cut in butter by hand or in food processor until mixture is even-textured. (Mixture will resemble fine meal as in pie crust). Mix in currants. Beat eggs with whisk until pale. Whisk in whipping cream. Add to batter. Knead by hand until soft ball is formed.

Roll out on floured board to ½-inch thickness, adding only enough flour to keep from sticking. Fold dough into thirds, and roll out again to ½ inch. Repeat folding and rolling dough. Roll dough to ¾-inch thickness. Cut with 3-inch round cutter.

Bake at 350 degrees 15 to 18 minutes or until light golden brown. Makes 12 to 14 (3-inch) scones.

❖

BULLOCK'S POPOVERS

Gargantuan popovers from Bullock's department store restaurants have been accorded rave reviews from hundreds of satisfied customers–and readers. For best results, use traditional deep popover pans that have been well seasoned.

> *6 eggs*
> *2 cups milk*
> *2 cups flour*
> *¾ teaspoon salt*
> *6 tablespoons butter or margarine*

Bullock's Popovers (continued)

Beat eggs in bowl. Beat in milk until blended. Combine flour and salt. Work butter into flour mixture. Gradually add flour mixture to egg mixture and blend well. Fill 8 generously greased or well-oiled custard or popover cups. Place cups on baking sheet and bake at 400 degrees about 1 hour or until golden. Makes 8 popovers.

Note: If using new custard or popover cups, season to prevent sticking. Cups should be greased and placed in hot oven 30 minutes. Remove grease and regrease cups before using.

❖

SANTA FE RAILROAD FRENCH TOAST

Readers have often requested this unusual French toast served for many years on the Santa Fe Railroad before disappearing from the scene. Pete Semerenko, a former conductor, tipped us off to the secret of soaking the bread overnight for convenience, but suggested that two hours was long enough to do a proper job. "The real secret is using whipping cream, not half and half, in the batter," Semerenko added.

5 slices day-old unsliced firm white or French bread, cut ³⁄₄-inch thick
6 eggs, lightly beaten
3 cups whipping cream
¹⁄₂ teaspoon vanilla
¹⁄₄ teaspoon salt
Shortening
Powdered sugar

Cut bread diagonally in halves. Beat eggs with cream, vanilla and salt until light. Dip bread into mixture and let soak at least 2 hours.

Melt shortening in pan to 1-inch depth and heat to 450 degrees. Add 3 or 4 bread triangles, or enough slices to fit pan without crowding. Fry until edges turn golden brown. Turn to cook other side just until edges brown. Remove and place on oven rack over baking sheet.

Bake at 400 degrees 3 to 5 minutes until puffy and golden. Dust with powdered sugar. Makes 5 servings.

❖

INDIAN FRY BREAD

The skillet bread is wonderfully simple to make and can be served like a tortilla with honey, beans or meat.

4 cups flour
2 tablespoons baking powder
1 teaspoon salt
½ cup lard or shortening
1 cup warm water
Honey
Oil for deep frying

Mix flour, baking powder and salt. Cut in shortening until mixture is texture of cornmeal. Gradually add warm water, using only enough to make dough stick together. Divide dough into balls the size of a fist. Cover with towel and let stand 10 minutes. Pat out to size of large pancake. Fry in deep hot oil until golden brown on both sides. Serve with honey. Makes 6 pieces.

❖

SPAGO'S PIZZA, CALZONE AND FOCACCIA

Wolfgang Puck of Spago in Hollywood shared his recipe for pizza dough that also is used to make calzone and focaccia. Several filling suggestions from Puck and his chefs will broaden your options with this popular bread.

SPAGO PIZZA DOUGH

1 package dry yeast
Lukewarm water
3 tablespoons sugar
2 tablespoons salt
5 ½ to 6 cups flour
¼ cup olive oil

Dissolve yeast in ¼ cup lukewarm water. Mix sugar and salt into 2 cups water in bowl. Place flour in mixing bowl. Add half of water mixture and mix with large wooden spoon a few minutes. Add olive oil and mix well. Add dissolved yeast mixture. Stir 1 minute. Add remaining water mixture to dough as needed. Remove from bowl and turn out onto floured surface. Knead until dough is smooth and elastic. Let rest 10 to 15 minutes before dividing into 8 portions for individual pizzas, 4 portions for medium pizzas, or 2 portions for 2 large pizzas. Makes enough dough for 2 small pizzas or calzones, 4 medium and 2 large pizzas.

SPAGO CALZONE

Spago Pizza Dough
Flour
2 cups shredded mozzarella cheese
½ cup cubed goat cheese
1 cup shredded Fontina cheese
2 small Japanese eggplants, sliced and grilled
2 ounces prosciutto
Virgin Olive Oil
Dash red pepper flakes
Dash crumbled dried basil
Grated Parmesan cheese

Pinch off 8 portions of dough. Using one portion at a time, let dough rest 10 minutes before using. Roll out to small circle, then stretch into circle about 12- to 14-inches in diameter. Distribute half of the shredded mozzarella slices and all of goat cheese, Fontina cheese, eggplant and prosciutto over dough circles. Top with remaining mozzarella cheese. Fold dough over to form half circle. Moisten edges to seal. Crimp edges.

Combine olive oil, red pepper and basil. Brush surface of dough with olive oil mixture. Bake at 450 degrees 15 to 20 minutes or until calzone become crisp underneath and golden brown on top. Sprinkle with grated Parmesan cheese, if desired. Makes 8 calzones.

SPAGO PIZZA

Prepare Spago Pizza Dough as directed for individual or large pizzas, as desired. Top dough circles with ingredients as directed for calzone or those suggested below. Do not fold. Bake at 450 degrees 10 to 12 minutes for small pizzas or 12 to 20 minutes for larger, depending on size, or until pizzas are crisp.

SUGGESTED FILLINGS FOR CALZONE OR PIZZA

Crumbled goat cheese

Chopped bufala mozzarella

Crumbled blue cheese

Crumbled ricotta cheese

Grated Parmesan cheese

Chopped cooked asparagus

Chopped cooked spinach

Tomato Sauce (1 tablespoon per individual calzone or pizza)

Chopped tomatoes

Sliced cooked mushrooms

Chopped artichoke bottoms

APPETIZER PIZZA

Prepare Spago Pizza Dough as directed for individual or large pizzas, as desired. Brush circles of dough with virgin olive oil. Bake at 450 degrees 10 to 12 minutes for individual pizzas or 12 or 20 minutes for larger, depending on size, or until pizzas are crisp underneath. While still warm, top each individual pizza with softened cream cheese. Layer with smoked salmon. Spoon small amount black caviar in center, encircle caviar with chopped egg then chopped onion. Sprinkle with finely chopped chives.

Spago's Pizza, Calzone, and Focaccia (continued)

FOCACCIA

Spago Pizza Dough
$\frac{1}{2}$ cup virgin olive oil
$\frac{1}{4}$ teaspoon red pepper flakes
2 teaspoons crumbled dried basil, rosemary, oregano or thyme
Grated Parmesan cheese

Prepare Spago Dough as directed for individual or large pizzas, as desired. Combine oil, red pepper flakes and basil. Mix well. Brush seasoned oil over each portion of dough. Sprinkle with Parmesan cheese. Bake at 450 degrees 10 to 12 minutes for individual or 15 to 20 minutes for large loaves, depending on size. Makes 8 small or 4 medium or 2 large loaves.

❖

LAVASH

Lavash, a crisp matzo-like cracker bread was popularized by Armenian-Middle Eastern groups. The cracker is ideal with soup or salad.

1 package dry yeast
1 tablespoon sugar
2 ¼ cups lukewarm water
6 cups flour
½ cup butter, melted
2 tablespoons sesame seeds

Combine yeast with 1 teaspoon sugar and ¼ cup lukewarm water in small shallow bowl. Let stand 2 to 3 minutes, then stir to dissolve yeast completely. Set bowl aside in warm draft-free place 5 to 10 minutes or until mixture almost doubles.

Pour flour into large mixing bowl and make well in center. Pour in yeast mixture, remaining 2 cups water, melted butter and remaining 2 teaspoons sugar.

With large spoon beat flour into liquid ingredients, continuing to beat 10 minutes or until soft spongy dough is formed. Cover loosely with towel and set aside in warm draft-free place until mixture doubles.

Place dough on lightly floured board and divide into 10 equal parts. Roll out each part as thinly as possible into circles, then place 2 to 3 circles on baking sheet.

Sprinkle lightly with cold water and sesame seeds. Bake on bottom rack of oven at 350 degrees 20 minutes or until pale golden brown. Transfer breads with wide spatula to wire cooling rack.

❖

SALADS & SALAD DRESSINGS

The West Coast has been a mecca for salad lovers. After all, California farms are the nation's largest supplier of fruits and vegetables year-round, giving restaurant and home cooks unlimited access to products.

Creativity knows no bounds and this chapter proves it. You will find a wide variety of vegetable, fruit, meat and poultry salads and dressings to go with them. We included old favorites, such as *Green Goddess Dressing* and *Thousand Island Dressing* as well as low- and nonfat dressings now in demand.

❖

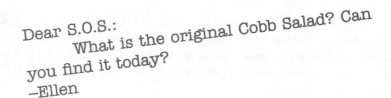

Dear S.O.S.:
    What is the original Cobb Salad? Can you find it today?
—Ellen

Dear Ellen:
    The salad made famous by the Original Brown Derby restaurant lives on in many guises. But the original formula— finely chopped greens, tomato, chicken, bacon, avocado, eggs and Roquefort served with French dressing remains king.

BROWN DERBY COBB SALAD

Cobb Salad was made famous by an equally famous restaurant, the former Brown Derby. There have been many impostors since, but Cobb Salad has remained king long after the original restaurant closed.

½ head iceberg lettuce
½ bunch watercress
1 small bunch curly endive
½ head Romaine
2 tablespoons minced chives
2 medium tomatoes, peeled, seeded and diced
1 chicken breast cooked, boned, skinned and diced
6 strips bacon, cooked and diced
1 avocado, peeled and diced
3 hard-cooked eggs, peeled and diced
½ cup Roquefort cheese, crumbled
Special French Dressing

Chop lettuce, watercress, endive and Romaine in very fine pieces. Mix together in large wide bowl. Arrange chives, tomatoes, chicken, bacon, avocado, eggs and cheese in rows over lettuce. At table pour Special French Dressing over salad, toss and serve. Makes 4 to 6 servings.

SPECIAL FRENCH DRESSING

¼ cup water
¼ cup red wine vinegar
¼ teaspoon sugar
1 ½ teaspoons lemon juice
½ teaspoon salt
½ teaspoon black pepper
½ teaspoon Worcestershire sauce
¾ teaspoon dry mustard
½ clove garlic, minced
¼ cup olive oil
¾ cup vegetable oil

Combine water, vinegar, sugar, lemon juice, salt, pepper, Worcestershire, mustard, garlic and oils. Chill. Shake well before using. Makes about 1½ cups.

HOTEL CAESER'S CAESER SALAD

The Caesar Hotel in Tijuana, Mexico, is said to have originated the Caesar Salad. This is their recipe.

3 cloves garlic
½ cup olive or corn oil
1 medium head crisp chilled romaine lettuce, torn
2 tablespoons wine vinegar
Juice of 2 lemons
2 eggs, coddled
Salt, pepper
Worcestershire sauce
6 to 8 tablespoons grated Romano or Parmesan cheese
1 ½ cups croutons

Place garlic cloves in oil in jar and let stand at least four hours before preparing salad. When ready to serve, discard garlic and add seasoned oil to greens in bowl. Add vinegar, lemon juice, eggs, salt, pepper and Worcestershire to taste, and Romano or Parmesan cheese and croutons. Roll as if folding (do not toss) salad until ingredients are well mixed. Makes 6 to 8 servings.

Note: To coddle egg, drop unshelled in hot, but not boiling water to heat, about 1 to 2 minutes.

❖

CAESAR SALAD

Because the U.S. Department of Agriculture cautions about the potential health risk of using raw (not cooked) eggs, we developed a recipe using egg substitute for the dressing of this ultra-famous salad.

Hearts of romaine
Egg substitute equivalent for 2 eggs
1 clove garlic, mashed
Juice of $\frac{1}{2}$ lemon
1 teaspoon salt
$\frac{1}{4}$ teaspoon dry mustard
$\frac{1}{4}$ teaspoon cracked pepper
Dash Worcestershire sauce
$\frac{1}{2}$ cup wine vinegar
6 anchovies, chopped
Oil
1 dozen toasted croutons
Grated Parmesan cheese

Wash romaine, pat dry and cut into $1\frac{1}{2}$-inch pieces. Chill.

Pour egg substitute into pint measuring cup. Add garlic, lemon juice, salt, mustard, pepper and Worcestershire. Blend. Add vinegar and anchovies. Fill measuring cup with oil, then blend carefully.

Pour enough dressing over romaine to thoroughly coat leaves. Toss and sprinkle salad with croutons and cheese. Makes dressing for about 10 servings.

❖

BULLOCK'S TRIO SALAD

Bullock's Wilshire Department Store has closed, but the Trio Salad lives on in countless readers' recipe files. The salads can be served separately or together.

BULLOCK'S FRUIT SALAD

1 ½ cups sugar
2 teaspoons dry mustard
⅔ cup vinegar
3 tablespoons onion juice
2 cups oil
3 tablespoons poppy seeds
Assorted cut fruit in season.

Combine sugar, mustard, vinegar and onion juice. Gradually add oil whisking until smooth. Add poppy seeds and blend well. Chill, covered in refrigerator. Add dressing in desired amounts over fruit. Refrigerate remaining dressing in tightly covered jar for later use. Makes about 4 servings.

BULLOCK'S CHICKEN SALAD

3 cups diced cooked chicken
¾ cup chopped celery
2 teaspoons salt
Dash pepper
1 cup mayonnaise
2 teaspoons seasoned chicken stock base
Lettuce

Combine chicken, celery, salt and pepper. Mix mayonnaise and chicken base and add to chicken mixture. Toss to mix well. Chill at least 1 hour. Serve in lettuce cups on a bed of chopped lettuce. Makes about 4 servings.

CRAB MEAT AND SHRIMP SALAD

2 cups shredded cooked crab meat
2 cups bay shrimp
1 cup chopped celery
2 teaspoons salt
1/2 teaspoon pepper
1 1/2 cups mayonnaise
1 tablespoons lemon juice
Lettuce

Combine crab meat, shrimp, celery, salt, pepper, mayonnaise and lemon juice. Toss until well mixed. Chill at least 1 hour. Serve in lettuce cups on bed of chopped lettuce. Makes about 6 servings.

❖

CHICKEN CURRY SALAD

We loved this salad the moment we tasted it at Butterfield's restaurant in Hollywood. Readers followed suit.

2 quarts water
1/4 cup sherry wine vinegar
3 whole chicken breasts, skin removed
1 large green pepper, diced
1 large Pippin apple, diced
3 large stalks celery, diced
5 green onions, green part only, sliced
1 cup mango chutney
1 cup plain yogurt
6 tablespoons mayonnaise, preferably homemade
1 tablespoon curry powder, preferably Madras, or to taste
1/4 cup raisins
1/2 cup sliced almonds
1 1/2 teaspoons freshly ground black pepper or to taste
Mixed baby lettuces

Chicken Curry Salad (continued)

Combine water and vinegar in large saucepan. Add chicken, bring to boil, then simmer over medium heat 10 minutes or until chicken is tender. Remove chicken from water and cool. Cut into cubes or pieces.

Mix together green pepper, apple, celery, green onions and all but 2 tablespoons chutney in large bowl. Add chicken, yogurt, mayonnaise, curry powder, raisins and almonds. Mix to coat chicken well. Add pepper to taste. Chill 1 hour.

Serve over mixed baby lettuces and garnish each serving with 1 teaspoon remaining chutney. Makes 6 servings.

❖

SCANDIA'S CHICKEN SALAD KON-TIKI

Another favorite from the now closed Scandia restaurant, this salad will remind you of Hawaii.

> **2 cups diced cooked chicken breast**
> **³/₄ cup diced crisp celery hearts**
> **Freshly grated coconut**
> **1 tablespoon mango chutney**
> **Curry Dressing**
> **2 cantaloupes or shredded lettuce**

Combine chicken, celery, ½ cup coconut and chutney and mix well. Toss with Curry Dressing.Cut cantaloupes in halves, remove seeds and fill cavities with chicken mixture. Or spoon chicken salad on shredded lettuce and garnish with cantaloupe or melon slices. Or dress salad by covering with dressing and arrange 3 slices of melon on top to form crown. Sprinkle with coconut. Makes 4 servings.

> **CURRY DRESSING**
>
> **½ cup mayonnaise**
> **½ cup sour cream**
> **1 teaspoon curry powder**
> **1 teaspoon lime juice**
> **Dash sugar**
> **Salt, pepper**

Blend together mayonnaise, sour cream, curry powder, lime juice, sugar, and salt and pepper to taste.

MADAME WU'S CHINESE CHICKEN SALAD

Sylvia Wu, owner of Madame Wu's Garden in Santa Monica said she had no idea the dish would catch on so quickly when she introduced this simple improvisation of an elaborate Chinese banquet dish.

2 quarts oil for deep-frying

8 squares won ton dough, cut in $\frac{1}{8}$-inch strips

$\frac{1}{4}$ (7- or 8-ounce) package rice noodles

1 head iceberg lettuce

2 cups diced or shredded cooked chicken, chilled

1 teaspoon prepared mustard

$\frac{1}{4}$ teaspoon five-spice powder, optional

1 teaspoon sesame oil

2 tablespoons light soy sauce

3 tablespoons finely chopped toasted almonds

$\frac{1}{2}$ cup thinly sliced green onions, whites only

Heat oil in deep fryer to 350 degrees. Fry won ton strips until light tan in color. Remove and drain on paper towels.

Divide rice noodles into 3 portions, Drop 1 portion into hot oil and cook just until noodles expand, becoming white and puffy. Remove instantly with slotted spoon. Drain on paper towels. Continue to cook remaining noodles, 1 portion at a time.

Shred lettuce and place on large platter. Chill.

Just before serving, combine chicken, mustard, five-spice powder, sesame oil, soy sauce, almonds and green onions in large bowl. Mix well. Add crisp-fried won ton strips and rice noodles and mix thoroughly. Noodles will break into small bits when mixed. Mound mixture over lettuce. Do not toss. Makes 4 to 6 servings.

Note: The dressing recipe can be doubled or tripled according to taste.

❖

CHART HOUSE SPINACH SALAD

The Chart House, and many other steak houses like this popular chain restaurant, started serving spinach salad as a healthful alternative to lettuce.

½ cup red wine vinegar

1 ½ teaspoons salt

1 tablespoon sugar

½ teaspoon dry mustard

1 teaspoon sweet pickle relish

½ teaspoon chopped capers

1 ½ cups vegetable oil

1 ½ teaspoons olive oil

2 hard-cooked eggs, peeled

3 bunches spinach

¼ pound bacon, minced

½ small onion, minced

¼ pound mushrooms, sliced

Blend vinegar, salt, sugar, mustard, pickle relish and capers. Stir in vegetable and olive oils. Set dressing aside.

Shred eggs on medium-size grater. Cover and set aside. Clean spinach, removing tough stems. Drain on paper towels and pat dry. Place leaves in large bowl.

Sauté bacon until crisp. Remove bacon and sprinkle over spinach. Add onion and mushrooms to drippings in skillet. Sauté until tender. Stir in 1 cup dressing. Bring to boil.

Pour over spinach and toss. Garnish with reserved shredded eggs. Serve with additional dressing. Makes 6 to 8 servings.

❖

Fromin's Tuna Salad

Fromin's in Encino serves a spicy delicatessen-type tuna salad that appeals to Angeleno's.

4 (6 ½-ounce) cans white meat albacore tuna, water-packed
3 stalks celery
2 slices egg bread
3 tablespoon sweet pickle relish
1 teaspoon white pepper
1 teaspoon garlic powder
1 cup mayonnaise, or to taste

Drain tuna well. Place in mixing bowl and break into small pieces.

Wash celery and chop fine. Trim and discard crust from egg bread. Finely chop bread.

Add celery, bread, relish, white pepper and garlic powder to tuna. Add mayonnaise and mix well. Cover and refrigerate. Makes 8 to 10 servings.

❖

Tabbouleh

When traveling to the Middle East became popular in the late seventies and eighties requests made tabbouleh, a healthful, low-calorie cracked wheat salad, a buffet star.

1 cup cracked wheat
4 bunches parsley, stems removed and finely chopped
4 green onions, finely chopped
4 sprigs mint, finely chopped or 2 teaspoons crushed dried mint
4 tomatoes, chopped
½ cup olive oil
¼ cup lemon juice
Salt, pepper

Place cracked wheat in large bowl with water to cover. Let stand 20 minutes. Drain and squeeze wheat dry in cloth towel. Place in large serving bowl. Add chopped parsley, green onions, mint and tomatoes. Mix well. Blend together oil, lemon juice and salt and pepper to taste. Pour over salad and toss to mix well. Makes 6 servings.

JULIENNE'S COUSCOUS SALAD WITH CURRANTS AND PINE NUTS

Julienne, a gourmet deli and café in San Marino, California, makes imaginative use of couscous, a staple of the North African diet. The grain can be purchased at most health food or Middle Eastern grocery stores.

2/3 cup dried currants

3 tablespoons unsalted butter

1/8 teaspoon powdered saffron

1 1/2 cups chicken stock

1 1/2 cups couscous

1 1/2 cups diced celery

1/3 cup thinly sliced green onions

1/3 cup pine nuts, lightly toasted

1/4 cup minced parsley

1/4 cup fresh lemon juice

1/4 teaspoon ground cinnamon

1/2 cup olive oil

Salt, pepper

Plump currants in warm water to cover 15 minutes, then drain and set aside.

In large skillet, melt butter with saffron over medium heat, stirring. Add stock and bring to boil. Stir in couscous, cover and remove from heat. Let mixture stand 4 minutes.

Transfer couscous mixture to glass bowl, breaking up any lumps with fork. Add celery, plumped currants, green onions, pine nuts and parsley. Toss to mix well.

In small bowl, whisk together lemon juice and cinnamon. Add olive oil in slow, steady stream, whisking constantly until emulsified. Drizzle dressing over salad. Toss and season to taste with salt and pepper.

Salad may be made 1 day ahead and stored, covered, in refrigerator until ready to use. Makes 6 servings.

❖

CANTER'S DELI POTATO SALAD

Canter's Deli on Fairfax Avenue in the heart of Los Angeles has been around for decades. Their potato salad is requested often.

> *6 potatoes, steamed until cooked through*
> *1 small onion, minced*
> *1 small stalk celery, diced*
> *1 small carrot, shredded*
> *½ cup mayonnaise*
> *1 tablespoon sugar*
> *Salt, pepper*

Peel and dice potatoes. Add onion, celery and carrot. Mix mayonnaise with sugar and season to taste with salt and pepper. Add to potatoes and toss to coat well. Makes 6 servings.

❖

NORTHWOOD INN'S RED CABBAGE SALAD

We have had an ongoing dialogue with readers trying to duplicate the recipe for red cabbage slaw from Northwoods Inn in Claremont, California. Some readers have helped with clues. Here is the recipe that we think is closest to the original, which is considered a trade secret by the restaurant.

> *½ head red cabbage*
> *2 teaspoons garlic purée*
> *¼ cup grated sweet red pepper*
> *1 small onion, minced*
> *2 tablespoons lemon juice*
> *3 tablespoons sugar*
> *1 tablespoon beef bouillon granules*
> *Salt*
> *¼ teaspoon black pepper*
> *½ cup wine vinegar*
> *½ cup cider vinegar*
> *1 cup oil*

Northwood Inn's Red Cabbage Salad (continued)

Shred cabbage into bowl. Combine garlic, red pepper and onion. Blend lemon juice, sugar, bouillon, salt to taste, pepper, vinegars and oil.

Pour over cabbage and mix well. Let stand overnight to mellow flavors. Makes 6 to 8 servings.

❖

LOW-FAT COLESLAW LIKE THE PANTRY'S

A reader asked for help in lowering the calorie, fat and cholesterol content from her favorite coleslaw recipe made at the Original Pantry, one of Los Angeles' oldest restaurants.

> *³/₄ cup low-fat mayonnaise or dressing*
> *3 tablespoons sugar*
> *1 ¹/₂ tablespoons white wine vinegar*
> *¹/₈ teaspoon garlic powder*
> *¹/₈ teaspoon onion powder*
> *¹/₈ teaspoon dry mustard*
> *¹/₈ teaspoon celery salt*
> *Dash black pepper*
> *1 tablespoon lemon juice*
> *¹/₂ cup imitation sour cream*
> *¹/₄ teaspoon salt*
> *1 large head cabbage, finely shredded*

Blend mayonnaise, sugar and vinegar. Add garlic and onion powders, mustard, celery salt, pepper, lemon juice, sour cream and salt. Stir until smooth.

Pour over cabbage in large bowl. Toss until cabbage is well coated. Cover and chill until serving time. Makes 8 servings.

❖

TOFU EGG-FREE SALAD

Tofu has become a well-liked soybean protein food many cooks have learned to use. Here is an example of how tofu became "egg-like" in a healthful salad.

½ pound fresh tofu or bean curd, cut in ¼- to ½-inch cubes
1 teaspoon sugar
1 tablespoon soy sauce
1 teaspoon minced green onion
1 teaspoon sesame oil
Lettuce, optional

Place tofu in large bowl. Add sugar, soy sauce, green onion and sesame oil. Toss lightly to coat well. Serve cold as salad with lettuce, if desired. Makes 2 servings.

❖

CLASSIC WALDORF SALAD

Readers still love this salad which was probably created at the Waldorf Hotel in New York ages ago.

1 cup seedless or halved and seeded red grapes
1 cup diced unpeeled red apple
1 cup diced celery
1 cup chopped walnuts
½ cup diced Swiss cheese
½ cup whipping cream, whipped
½ cup mayonnaise
1 teaspoon lemon juice
1 tablespoon sugar
8 to 10 apple cups or lettuce

Combine grapes, apple, celery, walnuts and cheese in bowl. Combine whipped cream, mayonnaise, lemon juice and sugar and mix well. Fold dressing into salad. Chill and serve in apple cups or on lettuce. Makes 8 to 10 servings.

Note: To make apple cups, cut off stem ends of apples and hollow out cups, using sharp knife. Brush generously with lemon juice. Wrap in plastic and refrigerate until ready to serve.

PERFECTION SALAD

Perfection Salad has been a standard buffet salad for almost a century.

> **1 (3-ounce) package lemon gelatin**
> **$1/2$ cup cold water**
> **1 cup boiling water**
> **2 tablespoons vinegar or Italian dressing**
> **$1/3$ cup finely diced celery**
> **$1/4$ cup finely diced green pepper**
> **$3/4$ cup finely shredded cabbage**
> **$1/3$ cup finely shredded carrot**
> **Salad greens**

Stir gelatin into cold water, then stir into boiling water until dissolved. Add vinegar. Chill until syrupy. Fold in celery, green pepper, cabbage and carrot.

Pour into well-oiled individual molds or one (1-quart) mold. Chill until firm. Unmold and serve on greens. Makes 4 to 6 servings.

❖

MOLDED CRANBERRY SALAD

Readers tell us that they remember their grandmothers making this salad.

> **1 envelope unflavored gelatin**
> **1 cup cranberry juice cocktail**
> **$3/4$ cup sugar**
> **1 cup whipping cream**
> **$1/2$ cup miniature marshmallows**
> **$1/2$ cup chopped nuts**
> **$1/2$ cup chopped cranberries**
> **$1/2$ cup well-drained pineapple tidbits**

Sprinkle gelatin over $1/4$ cup cranberry juice. Let stand 5 minutes. Stir over low heat until gelatin dissolves. Add sugar, remaining cranberry juice and whipping cream. Blend well. Chill until syrupy. Fold in marshmallows, nuts, cranberries and pineapple tidbits. Pour into 1-quart mold. Chill until firm. Unmold onto serving plate. Makes 4 servings.

OVERNIGHT FRUIT SALAD

This old-fashioned holiday salad never seems to age.

3 eggs, yolks, beaten
2 tablespoons sugar
2 tablespoons white wine vinegar
2 tablespoons syrup drained from pineapple chunks
1 tablespoon butter or margarine
Dash salt
2 cups miniature marshmallows
2 cups drained canned gooseberries or grapes
2 cups drained pineapple chunks
2 oranges, peeled and cut in pieces
½ cup whipping cream, whipped
½ cup sour cream
2 tablespoons chablis
Orange sections
Whole strawberries
Melon balls

Combine egg yolks, sugar, vinegar, pineapple syrup, butter and salt in top of double boiler. Cook over hot, not boiling, water until thick, stirring constantly. Cool thoroughly. Combine egg mixture, marshmallows, gooseberries, pineapple and orange pieces. Fold in whipped cream, sour cream and wine. Spoon salad into glass bowl and chill 24 hours or overnight. Just before serving, garnish with orange sections, strawberries and melon balls. Makes 6 to 8 servings.

❖

TAM O' SHANTER INN THOUSAND ISLAND DRESSING

Is there a dressing more versatile than Thousand Island? It goes on everything from hamburgers to a fancy Louis salad. Readers tell us that Tam O'Shanter's in Loz Feliz serves this excellent dressing.

½ hard-cooked egg, chopped
¼ cup canned chopped beets
3 tablespoons minced green pepper
1 teaspoon chopped black olives
1 ½ cups mayonnaise
1 teaspoon Worcestershire sauce
4 teaspoons chili sauce
1 tablespoon catsup
¼ cup tomato juice
Seasoned salt

Combine chopped egg, beets, green pepper and olives in bowl. Add mayonnaise, Worcestershire, chili sauce, catsup, tomato juice and salt. Mix well. Makes 2½ cups dressing.

❖

NO-FAT DRESSING

There is no end to requests for low- or no-fat dressings. We gave one reader two types to choose from.

1 (10 ½-ounce) can condensed beef broth
2 tablespoons chili sauce
2 tablespoons vinegar
1 tablespoon grated onion

Combine broth, chili sauce, vinegar and onion in jar with tight fitting lid. Shake well and serve over greens. Makes 1½ cups, or about 6 servings.

❖

PROUD BIRD HONEY MUSTARD DRESSING

The Proud Bird near LAX shared this very popular dressing.

3 cups mayonnaise
½ cup sugar
½ cup honey
¼ cup prepared mustard
¼ cup white vinegar
¼ onion, minced
¼ bunch parsley, chopped
1 cup oil

Combine mayonnaise, sugar, honey, mustard, vinegar, onion and parsley. Blend in oil. Chill about 1 hour before serving. Makes 5 to 6 cups dressing.

❖

HORIKAWA SALAD DRESSING

Many readers have requested this apple-flavored Japanese-style salad dressing. The chef at Horikawa, a Japanese restaurant in downtown Los Angeles, graciously shared the recipe.

2 cups cottonseed oil
¼ cup rice wine vinegar
3 tablespoons soy sauce
½ beaten egg yolk
2 tablespoons grated onion
⅛ apple, peeled and grated
1 tablespoon lemon juice
¾ teaspoon salt
¼ teaspoon pepper
¼ teaspoon dry mustard
½ teaspoon paprika

Combine oil, vinegar, soy sauce, egg yolk, onion, apple, lemon juice, salt, pepper, dry mustard and paprika in bowl or jar. Stir or shake well just before using. Makes about 3 cups.

NO-OIL DRESSING

Here's a very low calorie dressing made without oil that even Pritikin fans would approve of.

1 sweet red pepper, cut up

1 green pepper, cut up

2 medium tomatoes, cut up

1 bunch fresh basil

2 cloves garlic

⅔ cup pineapple juice

¼ bunch Italian parsley

⅓ cup raspberry vinegar

⅓ cup Dijon mustard

Dash dried thyme

Dash dried tarragon

Dash dried oregano

Dash white pepper

⅓ cup Worcestershire sauce

Combine peppers, tomatoes, basil, garlic, pineapple juice, parsley, vinegar, mustard, thyme, tarragon, oregano, pepper and Worcestershire in blender container. Blend until puréed. Refrigerate in air-tight container. Makes about 4 cups.

❖

GREEN GODDESS DRESSING

A waitress who once worked at the Velvet Turtle restaurant chain sent us this excellent Green Goddess Dressing.

2 cups mayonnaise

1 to 2 tablespoons anchovy paste

1 cup sour cream

1 ½ teaspoons spice blend or seasoned salt

3 tablespoons finely chopped parsley

3 to 5 cloves garlic, minced

½ medium onion, minced

½ teaspoon dry mustard

1 tablespoon tarragon vinegar

½ teaspoon celery seeds

½ teaspoon dried thyme

½ ripe avocado, mashed

½ teaspoon Worcestershire sauce

Few drops green food coloring, optional

Combine mayonnaise, anchovy paste, sour cream, spice blend, parsley, garlic, onion, mustard, vinegar, celery seeds, thyme, avocado, Worcestershire and food coloring in blender container. Blend until smooth. Makes 3¼ cups.

❖

SAUCES

There is something captivating about sauces because they represent the basis of many recipes. Without sauces, many dishes lose sparkle and verve. We give, in this chapter, some of the most sought-after recipes, such as spaghetti sauce, Greek garlic and yogurt sauces, salsa and even a low-fat mayonnaise to make at home.

❖

Dear S.O.S.:
     I love the mustard sauce served on grilled meats at Benihana's Japanese tepan restaurants in Los Angeles. Can you help with a recipe?
—Joe

Dear Joe:
     You're on.

CUCUMBER DILL SAUCE

Add dill to a cucumber sauce made with yogurt and mayonnaise and serve it with poached salmon or other fish.

1 medium cucumber, unpeeled
½ cup plain yogurt
¼ cup mayonnaise
2 teaspoons lemon juice
2 teaspoons grated onion
1 tablespoon minced parsley
½ teaspoon dried dill weed or 1 teaspoon chopped fresh dill
Salt, pepper

Grate cucumber and set aside. Combine yogurt, mayonnaise, lemon juice, onion, parsley and dill. Fold in cucumber. Season to taste with salt and pepper. Makes about 2 cups.

❖

BENIHANA'S MAGIC MUSTARD SAUCE

The Benihana chain of Japanese tepan restaurants serve this wonderful sauce on grilled meats. We suggest using it on steaks and roasts. Readers also ask for Benihana's Ginger Sauce which follows.

¼ cup dry mustard
¼ cup water
2 tablespoons whipping cream
½ cup soy sauce
1 tablespoon crushed sesame seeds
1 teaspoon grated lemon peel

Mix mustard and water in small mixing bowl to make paste. Stir in cream and soy sauce. Add crushed sesame seeds and lemon peel. Place in blender container and blend at high speed 3 seconds. Makes about 1 cup.

❖

BENIHANA GINGER SAUCE

3 ½-inch cubes peeled ginger root, chopped
½ cup soy sauce
¼ cup vinegar
1 large onion, sliced

Place ginger, soy sauce, vinegar and onion in blender container. Blend at high speed 2 minutes or until ginger and onion are minced. Makes about ¾ cup.

❖

SAMBI'S SAUCE FOR BROCCOLI

Sambi of Tokyo in Downey, California makes a sauce for broccoli using mayonnaise made from scratch. They offered a simplified recipe using store-bought mayonnaise for home cooks.

2 cups mayonnaise
2 tablespoons sugar
2 tablespoons soy sauce
2 tablespoons chopped parsley

Place mayonnaise in bowl. Add sugar and beat with wire whisk. Whisk in soy sauce and parsley. Serve over steamed broccoli or other vegetables. Makes about 2½ cups.

❖

RANGOON RACQUET CLUB CURRY SAUCE

The British Empire left it's mark with this outstanding curry sauce served at the now-closed Rangoon Racquet Club in Beverly Hills.

---

2 tablespoons peanut oil

1 medium yellow onion, minced

5 stalks celery, minced

3 cloves garlic, minced

2 ½ ounces curry powder

3 cups dry white wine

4 cups chicken stock or canned broth

1 cup shredded coconut

1 cup pineapple purée

1 apple, cored, seeded and puréed (or use applesauce)

½ pound raisins

3 ounces ginger root, peeled and grated

1 banana, minced

Arrowroot or cornstarch

Heat peanut oil in saucepan and add onion, celery and garlic. Sauté few minutes, then add curry powder. Continue cooking and stirring 5 minutes longer. Add wine and bring to simmer. Add chicken stock and simmer 15 to 20 minutes, stirring occasionally.

Spread coconut on baking sheet and toast in 400 degree oven until lightly browned. Add pineapple, apple, raisins and coconut to sauce. Cook 10 minutes longer. Stir in grated ginger root. Stir in banana. Heat until sauce is thickened stirring constantly. If necessary thicken sauce with arrowroot or cornstarch blended with a little water to make paste. Cool thoroughly then refrigerate for up to 2 weeks, using as needed. Do not freeze, as texture and taste will alter. Makes 2 quarts sauce.

Note: When ready to serve, add any cooked chicken, beef, pork or shrimp, allowing ½ cup cubed meat or shrimp per serving. Heat through and serve over hot cooked rice with condiments such as shredded coconut, raisins, chutney, banana slices, and peanuts.

❖

DISNEYLAND'S SPAGHETTI MEAT SAUCE

Disneyland is not only the home of Mickey Mouse. It is also the place where children enjoy this meat sauce for spaghetti.

> *2 tablespoons olive oil*
> *1 pound ground beef*
> *³⁄₄ cup chopped onion*
> *1 clove garlic, minced*
> *1 (1-pound, 12-ounce) can whole tomatoes*
> *1 (6-ounce) can tomato paste*
> *2 bay leaves*
> *1 teaspoon dried basil*
> *¹⁄₂ teaspoon salt*
> *¹⁄₄ teaspoon chile powder*
> *2 tablespoons chopped parsley*
> *2 tablespoons melted butter or margarine*

Heat oil and add beef, onions and garlic. Cook over high heat, stirring until meat browns. Add tomatoes, tomato paste, bay leaves, basil, salt and chile powder. Cover and simmer 30 minutes, adding water if sauce becomes too thick. Stir in parsley and melted butter. Makes about 5¹⁄₄ cups.

❖

FREEZER TOMATO SAUCE

Readers love to keep this freezer sauce on hand for omelets, spaghetti, rice, noodles, cooked roasts, meatballs or fried eggplant.

> *¹⁄₂ cup oil*
> *6 cups chopped onions*
> *6 cloves garlic, crushed*
> *6 green peppers, chopped*
> *6 stalks celery, chopped*
> *8 pounds ripe tomatoes, peeled, seeded and diced*
> *3 (6-ounce) cans tomato paste*
> *4 teaspoons salt*
> *¹⁄₂ teaspoon black pepper*
> *2 tablespoons brown sugar, packed*

Heat oil in large pan. Add onions, garlic, green peppers and celery. Simmer until tender. Stir in tomatoes, tomato paste, salt, pepper and sugar. Simmer, uncovered, 20 minutes or until tomatoes are tender.Stir occasionally.

Ladle into 1-pint freezer containers, leaving $\frac{1}{2}$-inch head space. Label, date and freeze. When ready to use, thaw overnight in refrigerator or about 2 hours in pan of hot water or defrost in microwave. Makes about 8 pints.

❖

LOW CALORIE MAYONNAISE

One solution for dropping calories in mayonnaise is to use gelatin instead of oil. Yogurt, too, serves as a substitute for high-fat oils.

1 teaspoon unflavored gelatin
$\frac{3}{4}$ cup milk
1 egg yolk
1 tablespoon vinegar
$\frac{1}{2}$ teaspoon salt
$\frac{1}{4}$ teaspoon dry mustard
Dash hot pepper sauce

Soften gelatin in $\frac{1}{4}$ cup cold milk. Add $\frac{1}{2}$ cup hot milk and stir until gelatin is dissolved. Beat egg yolk lightly with vinegar, salt, mustard and pepper sauce and stir into milk mixture. Chill until mixture begins to thicken, then whip with rotary beater. Store in refrigerator. Makes about 1 cup and yields about 12 calories per tablespoon.

LOW-CALORIE YOGURT MAYONNAISE

1 cup plain low-fat yogurt
2 hard-cooked eggs
2 tablespoons lemon juice
1 teaspoon celery salt
$\frac{1}{2}$ teaspoon dry mustard
$\frac{1}{2}$ teaspoon sugar

Combine yogurt, eggs, lemon juice, celery salt, mustard and sugar in blender or food processor, using steel blade. Process until smooth. Makes about $1\frac{1}{2}$ cups and yields about 15 calories per tablespoon.

PEANUT SAUCE

This sauce of Indonesian origin is served on satay (skewered barbecued meat), salads and noodles. It is made with peanut butter, a special Indonesian condiment called ketjap and spices, which can be found at any Asian grocery store.

1/4 teaspoon minced garlic
1/4 teaspoon minced onion or green onions
1/2 teaspoon ground coriander
2 tablespoons chile oil
1 cup water
1/3 cup peanut butter
4 teaspoons Indonesian ketjap
1/4 teaspoon chile paste or hot pepper sauce to taste
Salt

Sauté garlic, onion and coriander in chile oil. Add water and bring to boil. Stir in peanut butter and ketjap until smooth. Add chile paste. Season to taste with salt. Makes about 1½ cups.

❖

TAHINI

Sesame seed paste, called tahini is used to make this basic sauce to serve as a spread in pita sandwiches, or over meat, fish and vegetables.

> *2 cups sesame seed paste (tahini)*
> *2 cloves garlic, crushed*
> *Juice of 2 lemons*
> *Dash cayenne pepper*
> *Dash ground cumin*
> *Salt, pepper*
> *¼ to ½ cup water*

Combine sesame seed paste, garlic, lemon juice, cayenne and cumin. Season to taste with salt and pepper. Process in blender container until smooth. Add water to desired consistency. Makes about 2½ cups.

❖

TZATZIKI

Yogurt and cucumber dip is served at Greek restaurants, such as Papadakis Taverna in San Pedro, and in every Greek home. It's a wonderfully refreshing dip or spread for raw vegetables, pita bread sandwiches, hamburgers or grilled meats. We've also included a variation.

> *1 pint plain yogurt*
> *1 large cucumber*
> *3 large cloves garlic, crushed*
> *½ teaspoon salt or to taste*

Drain yogurt in cheesecloth-lined sieve overnight.

Peel cucumber and split in halves. Remove seeds and cut cucumber in chunks. Place yogurt in food processor bowl. With processor running, drop cucumber through feed tube into yogurt. Add garlic and salt. Mix well. Makes about 2½ cups.

❖

ZUCCHINI SALSA

When a reader requested a recipe for salsa made with zucchini to serve with roasts, chips or Mexican food, we turned a typical salsa cruda into zucchini salsa with great success.

3 small zucchini, thinly sliced

2 jalapeño chiles, stemmed, seeded, and minced

4 teaspoons olive oil

Juice of 1 lemon

½ teaspoon salt

¼ teaspoon black pepper

2 jalapeno chiles, stemmed, seeded, and coarsely chopped

2 large tomatoes, seeded and coarsely chopped

1 green onion, coarsely chopped

2 cloves garlic, minced

Juice of 1 lime

Combine zucchini, minced jalapeños, 1 tablespoon olive oil, lemon juice, salt and pepper in jar. Cover tightly and shake well. Let stand 1 hour. Strain.

Combine chopped jalapeño chiles, tomatoes, green onion, garlic, lime juice and remaining olive oil in food processor container. Process until finely minced, but not mushy.

Combine zucchini and tomato mixtures and blend well. Spoon into sterilized jars. Store in refrigerator. Makes about 2 pints.

❖

Cumberland Sauce

This sauce is a great idea for those who happen to have ham for a holiday feast—or even leftovers.

> *1 (30-ounce) can fruit cocktail*
> *¼ cup frozen orange juice concentrate*
> *¼ cup currant jelly*
> *2 tablespoons sherry or port*
> *¼ teaspoon ground ginger*
> *2 tablespoons cornstarch*
> *2 tablespoons lemon juice*

Drain fruit cocktail, reserving 1½ cups syrup. Combine syrup with orange juice concentrate, jelly, sherry or port, and ginger in saucepan. Heat until jelly melts, stirring occasionally.

Blend cornstarch and lemon juice until smooth and combine with jelly mixture. Cook, stirring constantly, until mixture thickens. Add fruit cocktail to sauce, heat 1 to 2 minutes and serve hot with ham. Makes 3 cups sauce.

Note: Sauce without fruit pieces added can be used to baste ham during last 15 minutes of cooking time, if baking ham.

> **QUICK CUMBERLAND SAUCE**
>
> *1 cup currant jelly*
> *1 (6-ounce) can frozen orange juice concentrate, thawed*
> *¼ cup sherry*
> *1 teaspoon dry mustard*
> *⅛ teaspoon ground ginger*
> *¼ teaspoon hot pepper sauce*

Break up jelly with fork and gradually stir in undiluted orange juice concentrate, sherry, mustard, ginger and hot pepper sauce. Mix well. Serve with cold sliced ham. Makes about 1½ cups.

Note: Sauce may be heated, and served over hot baked ham.

❖

EGGS & CHEESE

Even with a shift away from eggs and cheese, there are a few recipes from the *S.O.S.* archives that remain favorites. Readers simply won't part with *Mozzarella Marinara*, a scrumptious fried cheese dish covered with tomato sauce, from a famous celebrity-filled restaurant. Nor will they do without an occasional quiche, with or without crust. We added to this chapter only the recipes that have lived on and on.

❖

Dear S.O.S.:
      I would love a recipe for mozzarella marinara that is crispy and has a good sauce. Can you help?
–Cynthia

Dear Cynthia:
      This recipe from Valentino in Santa Monica fills the bill in every way. It's been a reader favorite for years.

VALENTINO'S MOZZARELLA MARINARA

This appetizer of fried mozzarella topped with tomato sauce has remained popular since it first appeared on Italian restaurant menus. One of the best came from Valentino's in Santa Monica.

---

12 (2 x 2 x 1 ½-inch) slices smoked mozzarella cheese
Flour
3 eggs, beaten
Bread crumbs
1 quart oil
Marinara Sauce

Coat slices of mozzarella cheese with flour on both sides. Dip mozzarella slices in beaten egg, a few pieces at time. Roll in bread crumbs until coated on all sides.

Heat oil in large skillet until hot. Add a few slices breaded mozzarella at a time, and cook until browned on both sides, turning once. Arrange on serving platter. Top with Marinara Sauce. Makes 6 servings.

MARINARA SAUCE

½ cup olive oil
2 large onions, coarsely chopped
3 large cloves garlic, minced
2 small carrots, peeled and coarsely chopped
2 anchovy fillets
2 (1-pound, 12-ounce) cans Italian plum tomatoes
Salt, pepper
8 basil leaves, julienned

Heat olive oil in 4-quart saucepan. Add onions, garlic, carrots and anchovies. Sauté over medium heat until onions are golden, 15 to 20 minutes.

Coarsely chop tomatoes and add with liquid to carrot mixture. Season lightly with salt and pepper. Bring to boil. Reduce heat and simmer 15 minutes. Strain sauce, returning liquid to saucepan.

Place strained mixture in food processor fitted with steel blade or in blender and purée until smooth. Return to saucepan. With liquid, add basil and blend well. Cook over low heat 20 minutes. Season to taste with salt and pepper. Makes about 4 cups sauce.

DEEP-FRIED BRIE

Skewered on a bamboo stick, fried Brie wedges make superb appetizers to pass around with drinks or as an appetizer course on a plate with jalapeño jelly and fruit. You'll notice that the recipe makes use of "panko," the Japanese light and airy bread crumbs used to coat batter-fried foods. You can, however, use any dry bread crumbs with good results.

6 bite-size wedges Brie cheese
Buttermilk
Flour
Panko bread crumbs (for tempura)
Oil for deep frying
Jalapeño-pepper jelly, optional
Curly endive leaves, optional
6 small bunches grapes, optional
6 strawberries, optional
6 orange wedges or slices, optional

Dip Brie wedges in buttermilk then coat with flour. Dip again in buttermilk and roll in panko until completely coated. Refrigerate until ready to use.

Heat oil to 375 degrees. Drop Brie in hot oil and cook until lightly browned. Do not overcook or Brie will melt into oil. Drain on paper towels. If used as first course, place cheese on upper half of plate with dollop of jelly on side. Arrange endive leaves on lower half of plate and top with grapes, strawberries and orange slices. Makes 6 servings.

❖

CLASSIC CHEESE STRATA

Bread and cheese leftovers go a long way in producing a wonderful and classic luncheon dish.

8 slices bread

4 slices sharp Cheddar cheese

4 eggs, beaten

2 cups milk

1 teaspoon instant minced onion

1 teaspoon dry mustard, optional

½ teaspoon salt

Green pepper rings

Pimiento, cut in strips, or crisp bacon

Cut crust from bread. Arrange 4 slices in greased 8-inch square baking dish. Place one slice of cheese on each slice of bread in dish, top with remaining bread slices. Mix eggs, milk, onion, mustard and salt until well blended and pour over bread. Let stand 10 minutes to absorb egg mixture, then bake at 325 degrees 45 minutes or until strata is puffed and golden brown. Garnish casserole with green pepper rings and pimiento strips or use crisp-cooked bacon slices. Makes 4 to 6 servings.

❖

REFRIGERATOR CHEESE SOUFFLÉ

When a cheese soufflé can be prepared ahead of time and refrigerated for as long as 24 hours before baking, you can bet it will be a favorite.

4 slices day-old bread

1 (7-ounce) jar pimientos

¾ pound sharp Cheddar cheese, shredded

3 eggs, beaten

1 ¾ cups milk

2 teaspoons brown sugar, packed

¼ cup minced green onions

1 ½ teaspoons prepared mustard

¼ teaspoon salt

½ teaspoon Worcestershire sauce

Remove crusts from bread and reserve. Cut bread into small cubes. Place half of bread cubes in greased 1 quart soufflé baking dish.

Cut pimientos in small pieces, reserving some for topping. Combine pimientos, cheese, eggs, milk, brown sugar, green onions, mustard, salt and Worcestershire.

Pour half of mixture over bread cubes in dish. Add remaining bread cubes, then remaining pimiento mixture. Make bread crumbs from reserved crusts. Top mixture with crumbs and reserved pimientos. Refrigerate 24 hours. Bake at 300 degrees 1 hour. Makes 4 servings.

❖

IMPOSSIBLE QUICHE

These are titled "impossible" because they are pies that make their own crusts. Readers love them.

10 slices bacon, fried and crumbled
$1/2$ cup chopped green onions
1 cup shredded Swiss Cheese
2 cups milk
1 cup buttermilk baking mix
4 eggs
$1/2$ teaspoon dry mustard
$1/4$ teaspoon salt
$1/8$ teaspoon white pepper

Sprinkle bacon evenly over bottom of lightly buttered 10-inch pie plate. Sprinkle green onions then Swiss cheese over bacon. Beat together milk, baking mix, eggs, mustard, salt and white pepper until smooth. Pour into pie plate. Bake at 400 degrees 30 to 50 minutes or until knife inserted near center comes out clean. Let stand 5 minutes, then cut into wedges. Makes 6 servings.

FISH & SHELLFISH

Health concerns are not the only reason our readers request seafood recipes. Fish dishes such as *Prawns Amaretto* from Hawaii, paella from a Spanish restaurant in Beverly Hills and salmon quiche from the Ahwanhee Hotel in Yosemite are strictly "I fell in love" dishes from restaurants. Other recipes have been in our *Dear S.O.S.* files for many years. A reader's grandmother sent her tuna casserole from the generation of the forties who cooked using canned food. All have enjoyed the respect and adoration of our readers.

❖

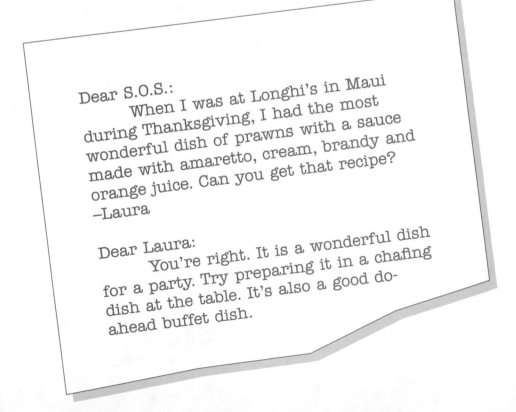

Dear S.O.S.:
    When I was at Longhi's in Maui during Thanksgiving, I had the most wonderful dish of prawns with a sauce made with amaretto, cream, brandy and orange juice. Can you get that recipe?
–Laura

Dear Laura:
    You're right. It is a wonderful dish for a party. Try preparing it in a chafing dish at the table. It's also a good do-ahead buffet dish.

SPAGO'S CRAB CAKES

Crab cakes from world-famous Spago restaurant are served on a bed of red pepper sauce created by chef Wolfgang Puck. If Louisiana blue crab meat is unavailable, any other type will do. Lettuce may be substituted for arugula, also known as rocket salad.

Olive oil
¼ red onion, diced
¼ large sweet red pepper, diced
¼ large yellow pepper, diced
1 cup whipping cream
¼ jalapeño chile, minced
⅛ teaspoon cayenne pepper
1 ½ teaspoons chopped chives
1 ½ teaspoons chopped Italian parsley
1 to 2 sprigs thyme, leaves only
1 cup bread crumbs
1 cup almond meal
Salt
1 extra large egg, lightly beaten
1 ¼ pounds Louisiana blue crab meat
Butter
¼ cup balsamic vinegar
Pepper
1 pound arugula
Red Pepper Sauce

Heat 1½ tablespoons olive oil in skillet. Add onion and peppers and sauté until onions are translucent. Cool.

Simmer cream with chile over medium-high heat until reduced to about ½ cup. Cool.

Pour cooled cream into onion mixture. Stir in cayenne, chives, parsley, thyme, ⅓ cup bread crumbs, ⅓ cup almond meal and salt to taste. Add beaten egg. Add crab meat and mix thoroughly. Combine remaining crumbs and almond meal on plate. Shape crab mixture into 12 small round cakes. Coat each side with bread crumb mixture and chill 2 hours.

Just before serving, sauté crab cakes in about 2 tablespoons hot oil and 1 tablespoon butter 4 minutes on each side. Drain on paper towels.

Spago's Crab Cakes (continued)

Mix ¼ cup olive oil with balsamic vinegar and salt and pepper to taste. Toss with arugula. Place salad in center of each plate. Pour Red Pepper Sauce around and place 2 crab cakes on top. Makes 6 servings.

Note: To make almond meal, process almonds until powdered.

RED PEPPER SAUCE

5 tablespoons butter
½ red onion, diced
½ large sweet red pepper, diced
2 cloves garlic, mashed
2 sprigs thyme, leaves only
½ cup white wine
1 cup whipping cream
Salt, pepper
Juice of ½ lemon

Heat 3 tablespoons butter in saucepan until foamy. Sauté onion, pepper, garlic and thyme until vegetables are tender. Deglaze pan with white wine and reduce until thick. Add cream, bring to boil then puree in blender. Add remaining 2 tablespoons butter, salt and pepper to taste and lemon juice. Strain and keep warm.

❖

CRAB ENCHILADAS

These Acapulco Restaurant Crab Enchiladas have been a favorite of Los Angeles Times readers for more than a decade. If you can't find fresh tomatillos, use canned tomatillos.

6 corn tortillas
Oil or lard
1 ½ cups crab meat
6 tablespoons minced onion
Salsa Con Tomatillos
Shredded Jack cheese
Sour Cream Sauce
Pitted black olives
Avocado slices
Sliced peeled tomatoes

Heat tortillas, one at a time, in oil until soft. Place ¼ cup crab meat in center of each, then sprinkle with 1 tablespoon onion. Spread a little Salsa Con Tomatillos on top. Roll tortillas and place, seam side down, in shallow baking dish. Cover with remaining Salsa Con Tomatillos. Sprinkle generously with cheese. Bake at 400 degrees about 10 minutes or until hot and cheese is melted. Serve with dollop of Sour Cream Sauce and garnish with olives, avocado and tomato slices. Makes 6 enchiladas.

SALSA CON TOMATILLOS

2 dozen tomatillos
Water
Oil
2 jalapeño chiles, stemmed, seeded and chopped
½ cup chopped onion
2 tablespoons chopped cilantro
1 clove garlic
1 teaspoon salt
2 corn tortillas

Remove papery husks from tomatillos, cover with water and boil until soft. Drain off half of liquid. Turn into blender and blend until smooth.

Crab Enchiladas (continued)

Meanwhile, heat $\frac{1}{4}$ cup oil in saucepan, add chiles and onion and cook until soft but not browned. Add cilantro and garlic, which has been mashed with salt. Cook 5 minutes. Add tomatillos. Fry tortillas in oil and place in blender with a little water and blend until smooth. Add to sauce and cook 5 minutes.

Note: For canned tomatillos, drain half of liquid and blend.

SOUR CREAM SAUCE

$\frac{1}{4}$ teaspoon minced garlic
$\frac{1}{2}$ teaspoon salt
1 cup sour cream
2 tablespoons chopped onion
2 tablespoons chopped cilantro
Dash sugar

Mash garlic in salt. Combine sour cream, onion, cilantro, garlic and sugar and stir gently.

❖

GAGE & TOLLNER CRAB MEAT DEWEY

A descendant of the Admiral George Dewey family is actually the owner of Gage & Tollner in Brooklyn, New York. The owner's wife, Gertrude Dewey, who also acts as chef occasionally, sent us the recipe for their crab meat casserole.

3 tablespoons butter or margarine
3 tablespoons flour
2 cups hot milk
Salt, pepper
1 small parboiled green pepper, cut into $\frac{1}{2}$ inch squares
1 pimiento, cut into $\frac{1}{2}$ inch squares
2 (6 $\frac{1}{2}$-ounce) cans crab meat
1 cup shredded Cheddar cheese
$\frac{1}{4}$ cup bread crumbs

Melt butter in medium saucepan. Stir in flour until smooth. Gradually stir in hot milk. Cook and stir until mixture thickens. Season to taste with salt and pepper. Gently fold in green pepper, pimiento and crab meat. Spoon into individual ramekins. Mix cheese with bread crumbs. Sprinkle over ramekins. Bake at 350 degrees 15 minutes or until bubbly and cheese melts. Makes 4 to 6 entrée or 8 appetizer servings.

❖

Prawns Amaretto

The treatment of prawns, in wine flavored with orange, was a pleasant surprise from Longhi's in Lahaina, Maui.

4 large prawns
Flour
1 tablespoon butter
1 tablespoon brandy
1 tablespoon Amaretto
Dash dry white wine
1 teaspoon orange juice
1/8 teaspoon grated orange peel
1 tablespoon whipping cream
1 teaspoon chopped parsley

Coat prawns with flour. Melt butter in small skillet. Add prawns and sauté until browned on both sides. Remove from pan. Add brandy, Amaretto, wine, orange juice and peel. Cook, stirring until liquid is shiny and slightly reduced. Add cream to sauce. Heat until sauce is slightly thickened. Add prawns. Sprinkle with parsley. Makes 1 serving.

❖

GENGHIS COHEN'S CRACKERJACK SHRIMP

When the craving for these incredibly tasty fried shrimp tidbits struck, nothing stopped a reader from weathering incredibly slow cross-town L.A. traffic to sit down to a plate of them at Genghis Cohen's restaurant in Hollywood.

1 pound medium shrimp (41-50)
Marinade for Shrimp
1 cup cornstarch
2 cups cottonseed or peanut oil
Ginger Sauce
2 cups shredded lettuce

Shell and devein shrimp. Rinse in cold water and pat dry. Place shrimp in Marinade for Shrimp, 30 minutes.

Place cornstarch in bowl. Coat shrimp well with cornstarch, using colander to shake excess cornstarch from shrimp.

Heat wok until very hot, then add oil. Heat to 375 degrees. Drop half of shrimp into hot oil and cook 2 minutes. Remove with strainer and drain on paper towels. Add remaining shrimp. Cook until golden. Drain.

Drain oil from wok (reserving for future use). Place Ginger Sauce in hot wok. Bring to boil. Add shrimp and toss to coat evenly with sauce. Pour shrimp mixture over lettuce. Makes 6 servings.

MARINADE FOR SHRIMP

1 tablespoon Shaoshing wine or sherry
½ teaspoon salt
1 small egg white, beaten
1 tablespoon cornstarch
1 ½ teaspoons oil

Combine wine, salt, beaten egg white, cornstarch and oil.

❖

GINGER SAUCE

1 tablespoon catsup
1 tablespoon chicken broth
2 tablespoons sugar
½ teaspoon chili sauce
3 cloves garlic, thinly sliced
½ teaspoon chopped ginger

Combine catsup, chicken broth, sugar, chili sauce, garlic and ginger.

❖

TEMPURA

Little Tokyo in Los Angeles was the source for this crisp and airy tempura. The Tentsuyu dipping sauce is great on steamed vegetables as well.

1 egg, lightly beaten
1 cup very cold water
1 cup flour
¼ teaspoon baking powder
Salt
Green beans
Carrot sticks
Eggplant slices
Sweet potato slices
Shrimp
Sea bass pieces
Oil for deep frying
Tentsuyu

Combine egg and cold water and blend well. Gradually add flour, mixing just enough to moisten. Stir in baking powder and dash of salt. Pat vegetables dry. Dip vegetables and seafood, as desired, into batter, allowing excess batter to drain off before adding to hot oil. Fry a few ingredients at a time in deep oil heated to 340 to 360 degrees, until pale golden. Drain on wire rack or paper towels before serving. Dip into Tentsuyu, served in small individual bowls. Makes 4 servings.

Tempura (continued)

Note: Do not let batter stand at room temperature too long or it will become too thick.

TENTSUYU

1 cup water
½ cup soy sauce
½ cup mirin (sweet rice wine)
½ cup flaked dried bonito
Grated daikon (white radish), optional

Combine water, soy sauce, mirin and dried bonito in saucepan and bring to boil. Remove from heat and add daikon to taste. Makes about 2½ cups.

❖

MAHI MAHI TERIYAKI

Mahi-Mahi became a favorite fish choice once it became common for restaurants to fly fish in on a daily basis. Here's a great treatment for this exotic fish from Hawaii.

1 pound mahi-mahi fillets
¾ cup soy sauce
¼ cup sugar
¾ cup sake

Cut fillets into small serving-size pieces. Combine soy sauce, sugar and sake in shallow dish. Add fish and marinate about 30 minutes. Remove fish from marinade and place on broiler rack about 4 inches from source of heat. Broil about 4 minutes on each side, basting frequently with marinade. Serve hot, sprinkled with some of warmed marinade. Makes 3 to 4 servings.

❖

GOURMET 88 SWEET-AND-PUNGENT SHRIMP

Living on the Pacific Rim, readers have access to numerous restaurants serving great Asian food. This recipe from Gourmet 88 in Burbank, California responded to numerous requests for their sweet and sour shrimp. You can use chicken, pork or beef cut into bite-size pieces in place of shrimp.

1 ½ pounds peeled shrimp
1 egg white
1 teaspoon salt
1 teaspoon white wine
Cornstarch
Oil for deep frying
2 green onions, chopped
Pungent Sauce

Clean shrimp and pat dry. Beat egg white (save egg yolk for another use) and add salt, wine and 1½ teaspoons cornstarch. Add shrimp and turn to coat well. Marinate at least 30 minutes. Lightly coat shrimp in additional cornstarch. Heat oil for deep frying until hot. Add shrimp and cook until shrimp is golden brown and crisp. Remove shrimp and drain.

Clean pan. Add 2 tablespoons oil and heat until hot. Add chopped green onions and Pungent Sauce. Add shrimp and toss until heated through and well coated with sauce. Makes 6 servings.

PUNGENT SAUCE

1 ½ teaspoons chopped onion
½ teaspoon chopped garlic
½ teaspoon chopped ginger root
½ teaspoon hot chile paste
2 tablespoons catsup
2 tablespoons lemon juice
3 tablespoons sugar
2 tablespoons vinegar
¼ teaspoon salt

Combine onion, garlic, ginger root, chile paste, catsup, lemon juice, sugar, vinegar and salt. Mix well. Makes about ⅔ cup.

CAJUN CATFISH WITH MARGARITA LIME SAUCE

The Whiskey Creek at Mammoth Lakes credits Paul Prudhomme for the hot, hot Cajun seasonings used in this recipe. You can cut down the fiery seasoning if you have a tame palate.

1/4 cup bacon fat or peanut oil
6 (6- to 8-ounce) fillets catfish
Cajun Seasoning Mix
Margarita Lime Sauce
2 limes, sliced

Heat bacon fat in skillet. Coat catfish fillets with Cajun Seasoning Mix. As fat begins to smoke, carefully place fillets in skillet using long-handled spatula. When coating blackens, turn and cook fish on other side until somewhat charred and fish is cooked through. If fillets are thick, reduce heat to cook fish through without scorching.

Place fillets on serving platter. Top with Margarita Lime Sauce. Garnish with lime slices. Makes 6 servings.

CAJUN SEASONING MIX

2 tablespoons to 1/4 cup Spanish paprika
1 to 1 1/2 teaspoons salt
1 to 1 1/2 teaspoons seasoned salt
1 to 1 1/2 teaspoons garlic powder
1 to 1 1/2 teaspoons onion powder
1 to 1 1/2 teaspoons cayenne pepper
1 to 1 1/2 teaspoons white pepper
1 to 1 1/2 teaspoons black pepper
1 to 1 1/2 teaspoons dried leaf thyme
1 to 1 1/2 teaspoons crushed, dried oregano
1 tablespoon sugar

Combine paprika, salt, seasoned salt, garlic powder, onion powder, cayenne, white pepper, black pepper, thyme, oregano and sugar. Mix well until blended.

MARGARITA LIME SAUCE

¼ cup tequila
½ cup sweet-and-sour bar mix
2 tablespoons triple sec
1 ½ teaspoons cornstarch
1 tablespoon finely chopped cilantro

Combine tequila, sweet-and-sour bar mix, triple sec and cornstarch in saucepan, stirring until cornstarch is well blended. Heat until slightly syrupy and translucent, stirring constantly. Just before serving add cilantro.

❖

KNUDSEN'S SALMON PARTY LOAF

We once mislaid this recipe from an old Knudsen Dairy booklet which readers often requested. A former Knudsen employee, who still had the booklet, sent us the replacement.

2 tablespoons unflavored gelatin
¼ cup cold water
½ cup milk
1 egg, separated
¼ teaspoon salt
1 teaspoon dry mustard
1 tablespoon lemon juice
2 tablespoons minced green pepper
¼ cup chili sauce
1 tablespoon minced onion
1 ½ cups cottage cheese
1 (7 ¾-ounce) can salmon, drained
½ cup whipping cream
4 strips green pepper
4 strips pimiento

Soften gelatin in cold water then dissolve in heated milk. Combine slowly with lightly beaten yolk. Cook over low heat, stirring constantly until mixture thickens.

Knudsen's Salmon Party Loaf (continued)

Add salt, mustard, lemon juice, green pepper and chili sauce. Cool.

Stir in onion and cottage cheese. Flake salmon and remove any bones or membranes. Add to cottage cheese mixture. Chill until slightly thickened. Beat egg white until stiff. Fold into salmon mixture. Whip cream and fold into mixture. Pour into 1-quart loaf pan. Chill until firm. Unmold and garnish with green pepper and pimiento strips. Makes 4 to 6 servings.

❖

LA MASIA'S PAELLA CALIFORNIA

Juan Jose, the original chef-owner of La Masia in Beverly Hills, suggests you vary the combination of chicken, meats and shellfish to suit your taste.

½ cup olive oil

1 (2-pound) chicken cut in 12 pieces

1 (1 ½ to 2-pound) lobster or small lobster tails, optional

¼ pound lean boneless pork, cut in 1/2-inch cubes

½ pound Spanish chorizo

1 large onion, cut in julienne strips

1 large red or green pepper, cut in thin strips

2 medium tomatoes, chopped

1 tablespoon finely chopped garlic

½ cup chopped parsley

3 cups long or short-grain rice

6 cups boiling chicken broth

¼ teaspoon ground saffron

½ teaspoon black pepper

Salt

12 clams or cherrystone clams

12 small or medium shrimp

½ pound scallops

½ pound crab legs with shell, cut in 1-inch pieces

½ cup cooked peas

½ cup chopped roasted fresh or canned pimiento

12 lemon wedges

Parsley sprigs

Heat olive oil in paella pan or 12- to 14-inch skillet or flat, flame-proof casserole. Add chicken and sauté until browned, turning often. Remove chicken and keep warm. Add lobster to pan and sauté 3 to 4 minutes or until golden brown. Remove from pan and keep warm. Add pork to pan and sauté 4 minutes or until browned. Remove pork and keep warm. Add chorizo and sauté until browned. Remove and keep warm.

For paella tomato base (sofrito), add onion and red pepper to remaining oil in pan. Sauté 3 minutes or until tender. Add tomatoes, garlic and parsley. Cook until slightly thickened. Add rice. Cook until grains are translucent. Add boiling broth, saffron, pepper and season to taste with salt, stirring well. Place chicken, lobster, pork, chorizo, clams, shrimp, scallops and crab over rice. Reduce heat and simmer, covered, 30 minutes or until rice is tender but firm. Do not stir paella after it starts cooking.

Remove from heat. Add peas and pimientos. Cover loosely with foil. Let stand 8 to 10 minutes. Garnish with lemon wedges and parsley. Makes 12 servings.

TUNA CASSEROLE

There are literally hundreds of versions of this good, classic American tuna casserole, with each cook adding a personal touch—anything from caviar to refrigerator leftovers.

1 (10 ½-ounce) can mushroom soup

¾ cup milk

½ cup mayonnaise

2 (7-ounce) cans tuna, drained

1 (10-ounce) package frozen peas, thawed

2 cups thinly sliced celery

2 hard-cooked eggs, peeled and sliced

½ cup sliced ripe olives

2 teaspoons dried oregano

½ cup crushed potato chips or corn flakes

2 tablespoons melted butter or margarine

¼ teaspoon salt

⅓ cup grated Parmesan cheese, optional

2 tablespoons minced parsley

Mix soup, milk and mayonnaise. Separate tuna into pieces and fold into soup mixture along with peas, celery, eggs, olives, oregano, half of potato chips, half of butter and salt. Turn into greased casserole, sprinkle with remaining potato chips. Drizzle with butter and top with Parmesan cheese. Bake at 350 degrees 25 to 30 minutes. Sprinkle with parsley. Makes 6 servings.

❖

LALA'S GUMBO

This recipe, originally printed in the old Los Angeles Times Home Magazine decades ago, has been a Food Section favorite since.

1/4 pound bacon, cut into 2-inch squares

2 pounds okra, cut into 1/2-inch slices

2 medium onions, diced

2 stalks celery, diced

4 cloves garlic, minced

1 (1-pound) can whole tomatoes

4 cups boiling water

2 bouillon cubes

Salt, pepper

3 tablespoons flour

1 cup cold water

1 1/2 pounds shrimp, shelled and cut into 1-inch pieces

Cooked rice

Fry bacon until crisp. With slotted spoon, remove to large kettle. Reserve bacon drippings. Sauté okra in half of reserved drippings, stirring constantly, about 10 minutes. Place in kettle with bacon.

Add remaining drippings to skillet and sauté onions and celery until onions are tender but not browned. Add garlic, mix well, then add 1 cup tomatoes. Cook, stirring occasionally, until tomatoes darken somewhat. Add remaining tomatoes and simmer 5 minutes. Add 1 cup boiling water, mixing well. Stir tomato mixture into okra mixture in kettle.

Add 1 cup boiling water to kettle. Add 1 bouillon cube and salt and pepper to taste. Stir over medium heat until gumbo comes to boil. Add 1 cup boiling water and remaining bouillon cube, reduce heat and simmer 20 minutes. Add remaining 1 cup boiling water, and cook 10 minutes.

Blend flour with cold water until smooth. Add to boiling gumbo and let come to boil again, stirring constantly. Add shrimp and simmer 5 minutes. Let stand 20 minutes before serving, or refrigerate overnight and reheat. Serve hot gumbo over rice in soup plates. Makes 6 to 8 servings.

❖

POULTRY

Eating less red meat and more chicken and turkey became the cry of the eighties. The result is an unusual mix of recipes one might find in the meat chapter, such as chili and steak. Instead, the chili is made with chicken and the steak is turkey steak. Another factor that has influenced the selection of recipes in this chapter is the population explosion of Asian and Latin groups. Our taste for hot and spicy foods has made Kung Pao chicken and chicken fajitas as familiar as hamburgers. Our new found appreciation of Southeast Asian flavors has enriched an already lush repertoire of favorite chicken recipes. Thai-roasted chicken and Thai chicken curry are a few examples. Moroccan Bastilla became a fad when club luncheons introduced this exciting savory phyllo pastry filled with chicken and eggs to *Dear S.O.S.* readers. Of course, there are the old time regulars–fried chicken, chicken with 40 cloves of garlic and herb roasted chicken to name a few.

❖

Dear S.O.S.:
    Do you have a recipe for chili made with chicken rather than beef?
–Lucille

Dear Lucille:
    Yes, and you can use turkey, if you like.

CHAN DARA CHICKEN CURRY

Chan Dara Siamese Kitchen was one of the first Thai restaurants to arrive in the Los Angeles area. Requests for their Chicken Curry followed soon after.

1/4 cup oil

1/4 cup red curry paste (kang pet dang)

2 teaspoons curry powder

1 chicken breast, boned and sliced

6 tablespoons fish sauce

2 potatoes, peeled and cut into 16 to 20 slices

2 carrots, cut into 16 to 20 slices

4 cups coconut milk

Heat oil in large skillet. Add red curry paste and curry powder. Stir-fry over high heat 1 minute. Add chicken, fish sauce, potatoes and carrots. Stir-fry until chicken is golden brown.

Add coconut milk and bring to boil. Reduce heat, cover and simmer 30 minutes. Makes 4 servings.

❖

THAI ROASTED CHICKEN

Readers who have learned to appreciate the wonderful aromas of ginger, garlic and coconut used in the Thai cuisine, truly enjoy this roasted chicken recipe.

2 (4-inch) pieces ginger root, peeled

12 medium cloves garlic

8 medium shallots

1 medium parsnip, peeled and cubed

1 cup canned coconut milk

1/2 cup dark brown sugar, packed

1/4 cup light soy sauce

5 tablespoons sesame oil

8 chicken breast halves or whole legs

1/4 cup cilantro leaves, minced

Thai Roasted Chicken (continued)

Mince ginger root, garlic, shallots and parsnip in food processor fitted with metal blade. Add coconut milk, brown sugar, soy sauce and sesame oil. Purée.

Pour purée over chicken and refrigerate overnight.

With oven rack at lowest position, bake chicken, uncovered, at 375 degrees 45 minutes to 1 hour, until topping is slightly dry. Place under broiler and broil until crisp and browned. Garnish with cilantro. Makes 6 to 8 servings.

❖

FUNG LUM'S LEMON CHICKEN

One of the fortuitous results of the opening of Fung Lum's restaurant overlooking Universal Studios in September of 1981 was the immediate onslaught of requests from readers for this recipe. You can substitute boneless pork loin or turkey.

1 pound boneless chicken pieces, cut in julienne strips

1 egg, lightly beaten

3 drops sesame oil

Cornstarch

Salt

Pepper

Peanut oil for deep frying

Water

2 tablespoons white wine vinegar

2 tablespoons lemon juice

⅓ cup sugar

2 drops lemon extract

In a large bowl combine chicken, egg, 2 drops sesame oil, 1 tablepoon cornstarch, 1 teaspoon each salt and pepper and toss until chicken pieces are coated and ingredients are blended. Deep fry coated chicken strips in peanut oil at 400 degrees until browned. Drain on paper towels. Cut into smaller pieces. Keep warm while preparing lemon sauce.

Blend together ½ cup water, vinegar, lemon juice, sugar, lemon extract, remaining 1 drop sesame oil and dash salt in wok or small saucepan. Heat to boiling. Blend together 1 tablespoon water and 1 tablespoon cornstarch until smooth. Stir into lemon mixture. Heat and stir until smooth and clear. Pour sauce over chicken and serve. Makes 2 servings.

FUNG LUM'S CHICKEN WITH CASHEWS

Another favorite from Fung Lum's.

½ pound boned chicken breast, cubed
½ egg white
1 ½ teaspoons cornstarch
2 cups water
¾ cup raw cashews
Oil
¾ cup diced celery
⅓ cup diced carrot
½ teaspoon salt
½ teaspoon sugar
½ teaspoon sesame oil
Shaoshing wine or sherry
2 cloves garlic, minced
2 green onions, chopped
1 (1-inch) piece ginger root

Cube or dice chicken. Stir egg white and ½ teaspoon cornstarch. Add chicken and toss to coat well. Set aside.

Bring water to boil in small saucepan. Add cashews and cook over medium high heat 5 minutes. Drain. Set aside.

Heat wok. Add 4 cups oil. Heat until hot. Add cashews and deep fry over low heat just until golden brown. (Do not allow to scorch.) Drain using colander set over large heat proof bowl to strain oil. Set cashews aside.

Return 2 cups oil to hot wok. Heat until hot. Add diced chicken mixture, celery and carrot. Stir-fry 2 minutes or just until chicken is cooked and vegetables are tender-crisp. Drain and strain oil. Set chicken mixture aside.

For seasonings, stir together salt, sugar, remaining 1 teaspoon cornstarch, sesame oil and 1 teaspoon rice wine. Return about 2 tablespoons oil to wok. Heat oil again. Add garlic, green onions and ginger root. Stir-fry 20 seconds. Add chicken-carrot mixture. Stir-fry just to heat. Add seasonings. Sprinkle with more wine if desired. Add cashews. Stir-fry few seconds. Makes 4 to 6 servings.

❖

HOT AND SPICY CHICKEN

Angelenos developed a taste for hot and spicy food from the Hunan region of China as new immigrants came to Los Angeles during the seventies.

1 pound boneless chicken
3 tablespoons regular soy sauce
Cornstarch
Oil
1 egg, beaten
Pepper
2 tablespoons chopped green onions
10 whole dry, hot red peppers
1 teaspoon grated ginger root
1 teaspoon chopped garlic
2 tablespoons black soy sauce
2 tablespoons sugar
2 tablespoons white vinegar
1 tablespoon white wine
¼ cup water
1 tablespoon sesame oil

Cut chicken into 2-inch pieces. Combine 1 tablespoon soy sauce, 1 tablespoon cornstarch, 1 tablespoon oil, beaten egg and pepper to taste in large bowl. Add chicken pieces and toss to coat well with soy mixture. Refrigerate at least 20 minutes.

Heat wok and add 4 cups oil for deep frying. Drop chicken pieces in hot oil and fry until browned. Remove chicken pieces and drain on paper towels. Remove oil from wok and store for other use.

Reheat wok, then add 3 tablespoons fresh oil. Add and stir-fry green onions and red peppers until onion is browned. Add chicken, ginger root, garlic, black soy sauce, remaining 2 tablespoons regular soy sauce, sugar, vinegar and wine. Stir-fry to blend flavors, then add 1 tablespoon cornstarch mixed with water and sesame oil. Stir until sauce is translucent. Makes 6 servings.

❖

NEW OTANI SAKE DUCK

Duck served with sake sauce at the New Otani Hotel in downtown Los Angeles intrigued numerous readers.

> *1 (2- to 4-pound) duckling*
> *Honey*
> *Grated peel of 1 orange or mandarin orange*
> *½ bunch green onions or 1 leek, finely julienned*
> *Sake Sauce*

Place duckling on rack in baking pan. Bake at 300 degrees 2 hours, basting with honey every 15 minutes. Remove from oven and cool to room temperature. Remove bones from duck and cut meat into desired slices. Sprinkle orange peel and green onions over duck. Pour Sake Sauce over duck. Makes 2 to 4 servings.

> **SAKE SAUCE**
>
> *1 cup mirin (sweet sake)*
> *½ cup soy sauce*
> *¼ cup orange juice*
> *1 teaspoon grated ginger root*
> *¼ cup brown sugar, packed*
> *1 tablespoon arrowroot or cornstarch*
> *1 leek, finely julienned*

Combine mirin, soy sauce, orange juice and ginger. Remove from heat and stir in brown sugar. Stir arrowroot or cornstarch with small amount of hot liquid until smooth and return to pan. Cook and stir until sauce thickens slightly. Strain sauce through fine strainer into another pot or sauce boat. Add leek to sauce and mix gently. Let stand 10 minutes to blend flavors. Makes about 2 cups.

❖

CHICKEN CHILI

Readers looking for a change from beef asked for chili with chicken. It worked.

2 tablespoons oil
1 small onion, chopped
2 to 3 cloves garlic, peeled and chopped
2 canned chipotle chiles, cut in thin strips
1 (14 ½-ounce) can chicken stock
2 to 3 tomatoes, coarsely chopped
2 cups diced cooked chicken
Salt, pepper
4 corn muffins, quartered
Shredded Jack cheese
Chopped cilantro
Lime wedges, optional

Heat oil in large saucepan over medium heat. Add onion and garlic and sauté until onion is translucent. Add chiles and sauté 1 minute longer.

Add chicken stock and bring to boil. Cook until liquid is reduced by half. Stir in tomatoes and chicken and simmer 10 minutes. Season to taste with salt and pepper.

Serve over quartered corn muffins in individual bowls. Top with cheese and cilantro. Garnish with lime wedges to squeeze over chili. Makes 4 servings.

❖

SPAGO'S CHICKEN WITH GARLIC

Spago restaurant in Hollywood gave garlic a good name when it shared this recipe with thousands of our readers.

2 (2-pound) chickens or 2 pounds chicken breasts
2 small heads garlic
Water
¼ cup chopped Italian parsley leaves
Salt, pepper
2 tablespoons unsalted butter
Juice of 1 large lemon
Blanched Fresh Vegetables, optional

Halve chickens and bone completely, except for wing joint, if using whole chickens. (Bone chicken breasts, if using breasts). Place garlic heads in water to cover in small saucepan. Bring to boil. Drain. Peel garlic and cut each clove into paper thin slices. Toss in bowl with parsley. Season to taste with salt and pepper.

Using about 2 teaspoons garlic mixture, stuff under skin of chicken. Reserve remaining garlic mixture. Set chicken aside.

Place chicken on grill over hot coals and cook 5 to 7 minutes on each side or until chicken is no longer pink. Do not overcook chicken.

Heat butter in skillet. Add remaining garlic mixture to pan. Sauté several seconds. Add lemon juice and season to taste with salt and pepper. Heat through. Place chicken on large heated platter. Spoon garlic-parsley sauce over chicken. Serve with blanched fresh vegetables, if desired. Makes 4 servings.

❖

SANTA MARIA BARBECUED CHICKEN

Using beer to simmer grilled chicken may sound like an unusual way to barbecue chicken, but it also keeps the chicken moist and tasty, the way the barbecue buffs at the Santa Maria rodeos like it.

6 chicken halves
Garlic salt
Pepper
1 to 2 (12-ounce) cans beer

Sprinkle chicken with garlic salt and pepper to taste. Grill over medium-hot coals until browned, about 30 to 40 minutes. Meanwhile, heat beer in pot large enough to hold chicken. Drop grilled chicken in pot containing simmering beer, cover and simmer 15 to 20 minutes or until chicken is very tender. Makes 6 to 12 servings.

❖

TAMALE PIE CASSEROLE

Readers who have a hankering for California-style tamale pie as comfort food are bound to receive comfort with this recipe.

1 (14 ½-ounce) can chicken broth
Water
2 ¼ teaspoons salt
1 ½ cups cornmeal
1 cup chopped onion
1 teaspoon minced garlic
1 tablespoon oil
½ teaspoon crushed oregano
1 (1-pound) can stewed tomatoes
1 (12-ounce) can whole-kernel corn, drained
1 tablespoon chili powder
2 cups cut-up cooked chicken or turkey

Combine broth with water to measure 2½ cups. Heat with ¾ teaspoon salt.

Mix 1¼ cups cornmeal with 1 cup cold water and stir into hot broth. Cook and stir until mixture boils and thickens. Reduce heat, cover and cook until very thick, about 10 minutes, stirring occasionally.

Cook onion and garlic in hot oil until tender. Add oregano, tomatoes, corn, chili powder and remaining 1½ teaspoons salt and simmer 5 minutes. Slowly stir in remaining ¼ cup cornmeal and cook until thickened. Add chicken.

Line 1½-quart baking dish with cornmeal mixture, reserving about 1 cup for topping. Add chicken mixture to baking dish. Spoon or pipe reserved 1 cup cornmeal mixture around edge. Bake at 350 degrees 20 to 30 minutes, or until heated through. Makes 4 to 6 servings.

❖

LOCO POLLO

El Pollo Loco, the highly successful grilled chicken fast food chain in Southern California, was not about to turn over its trade secret, so our test kitchen developed a facsimile of its delicious grilled chicken.

¼ cup corn oil

¼ cup melted butter

½ teaspoon onion powder

½ teaspoon garlic powder

1 teaspoon annatto powder or few drops yellow food color

¼ teaspoon ground cumin

2 teaspoons lemon juice

1 (2 ½- to 3-pound) chicken, halved

Beans

Rice

Tortillas

Salsa

Combine oil, butter, onion powder, garlic powder, annatto powder, cumin and lemon juice in large shallow pan. Add chicken halves, turning to coat well. Cover and marinate several hours or overnight.

Remove chicken from marinade, cook on grill over medium coals, or 4-inches from source of heat under broiler, until browned on both sides and meat is done, turning and basting frequently, about 25 minutes.

Cut chicken halves into pieces to serve with beans and rice, corn or flour tortillas and salsa, if desired. Makes 6 servings.

❖

ANTONIO'S CHICKEN MOLE

Antonio's Mexican restaurant in Los Angeles provided the recipe for this classic chili sauce–flavored with chocolate, tomato and spices–to go with chicken.

2 (2 ½- to 3-pound) chickens, cut up
2 dried California chiles
2 dried pasilla negra chiles (black pasilla)
2 long mild green chiles
½ cup peanuts
½ cup pecans
¼ cup walnuts
1 (3.1- ounce) tablet Mexican chocolate, cut up
1 banana, cut up
1 large tomato, peeled and chopped
½ onion, chopped
3 cloves garlic, minced
Dash ground oregano
Dash ground cumin
1 teaspoon sugar
Salt
Oil
½ small onion, chopped
1 medium tomato, peeled and chopped

Simmer chickens in boiling salted water to cover until tender. Drain, reserving 4 cups broth.

Meanwhile, soak dried California and pasilla chiles in warm water to cover 30 minutes. Drain and remove stems and seeds. Grind soaked dried chiles and green chiles in food processor or blender until puréed, adding small amounts of chicken broth or hot water to facilitate grinding. Strain chiles through sieve to remove bits of peel.

Combine chili pulp, peanuts, pecans, walnuts, chocolate, banana, large tomato, onion, 2 cloves garlic, oregano, cumin, sugar, 1 teaspoon salt and 2 cups reserved broth in large pot. Cook 15 minutes, stirring occasionally.

Pour mixture into blender and grind until puréed. Blend 2 teaspoons oil to mixture. Return sauce mixture to pot, add remaining 2 cups chicken broth and simmer slowly 30 minutes. Heat 1 tablespoon oil in medium skillet. Add onion and remaining clove garlic and cook until onion is tender. Add medium tomato and cook until tender. Add chicken and stir to mix. Season to taste with salt. Makes 8 to 10 servings.

SIZZLING CHICKEN FAJITAS

When Tex Mex was big, so were fajitas—especially with chicken. This recipe can be modified to use beef, pork or turkey, as well.

3 pounds boned and skinned chicken breasts
Marinade
1/3 cup butter or margarine
2 medium onions, cut into 1/4-inch slices
4 medium green peppers, cut into 1/4-inch slices
1 teaspoon seasoning salt
Achiote Sauce
1 pound tomatoes, cut in wedges
Lemon wedges

Place chicken in shallow pan. Pour marinade over and let marinate in refrigerator 3 hours.

Melt butter in large skillet. Add onions, green peppers and seasoning salt and sauté until vegetables are tender, basting with Achiote Sauce while sautéing.

Remove chicken breasts from marinade and cut into 3 x 1/2-inch strips. Place chicken in large cast-iron skillet and sear over medium heat. Remove from skillet when golden. Place another iron skillet upside down over flame. Heat almost to point of smoking, about 90 seconds.

Remove hot serving skillet from burner and pile with chicken strips and vegetables. Place tomato wedges over chicken and vegetables. Garnish with lemon wedges. Makes 6 servings.

MARINADE

2 1/2 cups soy sauce
1 1/4 cups water
1 1/4 cups white vinegar
1 teaspoon minced garlic
1 teaspoon white pepper

Combine soy sauce, water, vinegar, garlic and pepper in large container. Mix with wire whisk until blended.

Sizzling Chicken Fajitas (continued)

ACHIOTE SAUCE

4 ounces achiote powder
1 ¼ cups orange juice
1 teaspoon granulated garlic
Dash oregano

Place achiote powder, orange juice, garlic and oregano in blender container and blend until smooth.

❖

GREEK LEMON CHICKEN

Many Greek restaurants feature chicken roasted with lemon and herbs, just as it is in Greek villages.

2 whole chickens
1 cup lemon juice
3 cups water
1 cup olive oil
4 cloves garlic, chopped
1 teaspoon dried oregano
2 teaspoons garlic powder
Seasoned salt
Freshly ground pepper

Cut each chicken in quarters. Rinse and pat dry with paper towels. Combine lemon juice, water, olive oil, garlic, oregano and garlic powder. Mix well then season to taste with seasoned salt and pepper. Add to chicken and mix well. Marinate 1 hour.

Place chicken pieces in large baking pan. Cover with foil and bake at 450 degrees 45 minutes. Remove chicken pieces from sauce. Place chicken in another baking dish and bake at 550 degrees about 10 to 15 minutes until brown and crisp. Makes 8 servings.

Note: Recipe may be easily cut in half. Chicken may be baked with marinade in advance and left in sauce, then pieces may be lifted from sauce as needed and baked or broiled to brown.

DELMONICO'S SICILIAN HERB-ROASTED CHICKEN

A specialty from Delmonico's restaurant in West Los Angeles.

1 ½ large onions, diced
1 ½ oranges, peeled and diced
1 tablespoon minced garlic
1 tablespoon fresh rosemary leaves
1 ½ teaspoons minced fresh basil leaves
1 ½ teaspoons chopped parsley
1 ½ teaspoons chopped fresh thyme leaves
1 ½ teaspoons chopped fresh oregano leaves
1 (4- to 5-pound) chicken
1 ½ teaspoons ground dried rosemary
1 ½ teaspoons ground dried sage
1 ½ teaspoons crushed bay leaf
1 ½ teaspoons ground fennel seed
1 tablespoon dried, crushed thyme
1 ½ teaspoons white peppercorns, crushed
1 ½ teaspoons black peppercorns, crushed
1 ½ teaspoons kosher salt

Combine onions, oranges, garlic, fresh rosemary, basil, parsley, thyme and oregano in bowl. Mix and stuff into chicken cavity. Truss and let chicken stand 24 hours in refrigerator.

Combine rosemary, sage, bay leaf, fennel seed, thyme, white pepper, black pepper and salt in small bowl. Rub chicken all over with 3 tablespoons dry seasoning mixture. (Reserve any remaining seasoning mix for another use.) Bake chicken at 400 degrees 50 to 55 minutes. Cut chicken into quarters or halves to serve. Makes 4 to 6 servings.

❖

JAMAICAN JERK CHICKEN

Jerk meat dishes were originally created by maroons (escaped slaves) in Jamaica during the 18th century as a method of preserving pork by rubbing it with a chili paste then smoking the meat in an open pit. Later chicken also was rubbed with the same chili mixture, but grilled over low coals so it develops a rather dried out crusty top, similar to smoked meat.

¼ cup Caribbean hot sauce

2 tablespoons dried rosemary

2 tablespoons chopped parsley

2 tablespoons dried basil

2 tablespoons dried thyme

2 tablespoons mustard seeds

4 tablespoons chopped green onions

1 teaspoon salt

1 teaspoon black pepper

Juice of 2 limes

2 tablespoons orange juice

Vinegar

6 whole chicken legs

Combine hot sauce, rosemary, parsley, basil, thyme, mustard seeds, green onions, salt, pepper, lime juice, orange juice and 2 tablespoons vinegar in blender container and blend until paste is formed. Paste should be consistency of thick tomato sauce. If too thick, thin with more vinegar.

Cover and let stand in refrigerator 2 hours or overnight (but not more than 2 weeks).

Rub chicken with paste and grill over very low coals, uncovered, 1 hour. If covered, place coals to one side of grill and chicken on other and cook about ½ hour. Makes 6 servings.

Note: For turkey, use whole turkey or turkey parts. Brush paste as directed. Roast at 350 degrees according to time table for turkey. Turkey can be covered until almost done, then remove cover to allow skin and paste to crisp.

❖

CHICKEN TANDOORI

The tandoor, a clay pit oven used to bake poultry, meats and breads, which cling to its hot walls, is also the name of dishes made in the oven. Tandoor chicken dishes vary with every Indian cook. This one calls for baking in a conventional oven, however.

2 chickens, halved
2 large onions, chopped
2 green peppers, diced
2 tomatoes, chopped
1 tablespoon curry powder
1 tablespoon ground coriander
1 tablespoon ground cumin
1 teaspoon ground turmeric
½ teaspoon ground cinnamon
½ teaspoon garlic powder
1 teaspoon black pepper
Salt
½ cup butter, melted
2 cups water
Tomato slices, optional
Green pepper rings, optional
Celery stalks, optional
Hot cooked rice
Peanuts, sieved hard-cooked eggyolk, yogurt, chutney and
*   grated coconut, optional*

Place chicken in shallow baking pan. Sprinkle with onions, green peppers, tomatoes, curry, coriander, cumin, turmeric, cinnamon, garlic and pepper. Season to taste with salt. Add melted butter. Turn chicken to mix with other ingredients. Cover and marinate in refrigerator several hours or overnight.

Add water. Bake at 375 degrees 50 minutes. If desired, garnish with tomato slices, green pepper rings and celery stalks. Serve with hot cooked rice. Pass small bowls of condiments such as peanuts, sieved hard-cooked egg yolk, yogurt, chutney and grated coconut to sprinkle over chicken. Makes 4 servings.

❖

MARRAKESH BASTILLA

This Moroccan national dish is a terrific party dish that can be made the day or night before. This recipe comes from the Marrakesh Restaurant in Newport Beach, California.

1 (2-pound) chicken, cut up

2 cups chopped onions

1 cup chopped parsley

½ cup unsalted butter

Dash saffron

2 cups water

Salt, pepper

5 eggs, beaten

2 cups toasted ground almonds

1 cup sugar

1 ½ teaspoons ground cinnamon

Melted butter

6 sheets phyllo dough

¼ cup powdered sugar

Combine chicken pieces, onions, parsley, unsalted butter, saffron, water and salt and pepper to taste in large saucepan. Bring to boil. Reduce heat, cover and simmer 45 minutes or until chicken is tender. Remove chicken from pan and cool. Reserve broth. Remove meat from bones and dice. Set aside.

Place reserved chicken broth in skillet. Bring to simmer. Stir in eggs. Cook, stirring constantly to scramble, until eggs are cooked. Set aside. Combine almonds, sugar and ½ teaspoon cinnamon. Set aside. Above mixtures may be prepared ahead and refrigerated.

When ready to assemble dish about 1 hour before serving, brush 12-inch ovenproof frying pan with rounded sides with melted butter. Layer 3 sheets phyllo in skillet, brushing each sheet with butter. About 5 inches of dough should hang over edge of pan. Sprinkle ⅓ of almond mixture and ⅓ of chicken mixture over dough. Top with another ⅓ of almond mixture and ⅓ of egg mixture. Repeat layers until ingredients are used. Fold bottom sheets of phyllo over filling. Brush with butter. Top with remaining 3 phyllo sheets, brushing each sheet with butter and tucking ends underneath.

Bake at 400 degrees 15 to 20 minutes or until golden brown. Cool slightly, then invert onto serving platter. Sprinkle with powdered sugar and remaining cinnamon while still warm. Makes 6 servings.

Note: Don't be afraid to handle phyllo dough. Tears can be patched and even dry patches can be moistened with a light misting with water. Use phyllo dough as soon after purchase as possible. To prevent drying keep phyllo dough covered with a damp towel. If frozen, the dough should be thawed in the refrigerator.

❖

MEAT

Americans may not be eating as much beef as they once did, because of concerns over fat and cholesterol intake, but requests for old favorites never seem to wane. Where would we be without sticky bones, barbecued beef or chili? Readers, always on the lookout for a new spin on an old favorite, have introduced countless other readers to *72 Market Street Meat Loaf* created by California chef, Leonard Schwartz, now at Maple Drive in Beverly Hills. Other old favorites are here, too, such as *Steak Diane* and *Salisbury Steak*. Reader's taste for hot, spicy and novel foods is reflected in such recipes as orange beef and Indonesian *Satay*.

❖

Dear S.O.S.:
        I am desperately searching for a recipe for the commercial honeyed ham. The most common is very expensive. I want to serve this to about 60 people at a very special birthday party.
—Barbara

Dear Barbara:
        According to one of our readers, Laura Wang, this less expensive version of honeyed ham is close to the real thing.

SATAY

In Los Angeles, satay is often used as a convenient hibachi appetizer for summer patio or pool parties.

> *1 pound boneless lamb*
> *2 cloves garlic, minced*
> *1 onion sliced*
> *½ teaspoon black pepper*
> *2 tablespoons ketjap (Indonesian-style sweetened soy sauce)*
> *Butter or margarine, softened*
> *Satay sauce*

Cut meat into ¾-inch squares or strips 4- to 6-inches long, 1-inch wide and ⅛-inch thick. Place in bowl. Add garlic, onion, pepper and ketjap. Mix well. Marinate 1 hour. Weave strips on bamboo skewers, allowing one strip per skewer. Cook over coals, or place under broiler 6 inches from source of heat and broil 12 minutes, turning often. Brush meat with butter halfway through cooking. Serve hot with Satay Sauce spooned over meat. Makes 4 main-dish servings or 8 appetizer servings.

Note: To keep bamboo skewers from burning, soak them in water for several hours, or overnight before using, or wrap ends in foil.

> **SATAY SAUCE**
>
> *2 tablespoons oil*
> *2 medium onions, coarsely chopped*
> *2 cloves garlic, minced*
> *1 serrano chile, stemmed, seeded and minced, optional*
> *1 cup ketjap*
> *2 teaspoons lime juice*
> *⅓ cup creamy-style peanut butter*

Heat oil in saucepan. Add onions, garlic and chile and sauté until half cooked. Turn into blender or food processor and grind until fine. Return to saucepan and add ketjap, lime juice and peanut butter. Heat, stirring, until peanut butter melts.

❖

STEAK DIANE

Readers can be assured of a romantic dish for Valentine's day with this show-off dish that can be prepared without leaving the table.

¼ cup butter or margarine
¼ cup minced shallots or green onions
2 tablespoons Worcestershire sauce
¼ cup beef bouillon
½ teaspoon salt
⅛ teaspoon black pepper
2 (6-ounce) New York steaks, ½-inch thick
¼ cup brandy

Melt butter, then add shallots and cook until tender but not browned. Add Worcestershire, bouillon, salt and pepper. Bring to boil and cook until liquid is reduced by about half.

Meanwhile, pan-broil steaks until rare or done as desired. Transfer meat and sauce to chafing dish or leave in skillet. Add sauce to steaks and turn to coat well.

Warm brandy. Pour over steaks and carefully ignite. Let flames die down and serve at once. Makes 2 servings.

MEAT LOAF 72 MARKET STREET

The best meat loaf (readers will testify) comes from 72 Market Street, a restaurant in Venice, California. According to Chef Leonard Schwartz who developed the recipe, it was a result of years of experience, not just an experiment.

¾ cup minced onion
¾ cup minced green onion
½ cup minced celery
½ cup minced carrot
¼ cup minced green pepper
¼ cup minced sweet red pepper
2 teaspoons minced garlic
3 tablespoons butter
1 teaspoon salt
¼ teaspoon cayenne pepper
1 teaspoon black pepper
½ teaspoon white pepper
½ teaspoon ground cumin
½ teaspoon ground nutmeg
½ cup half and half
½ cup catsup
1 ½ pounds lean ground beef
½ pound lean ground pork
3 eggs, beaten
¾ cup dry bread crumbs
Sauce

Sauté onion, green onion, celery, carrot, green pepper, red pepper and garlic in butter until vegetables are soft and liquid is evaporated. Set aside to cool.

Combine salt, cayenne, black pepper, white pepper, cumin and nutmeg and add to vegetable mixture. Stir in half and half, catsup, beef, pork, eggs and bread crumbs. Mix well.

Form into loaf and place on greased baking sheet or in 9 x 5-inch loaf pan. Bake at 350 degrees 45 to 50 minutes. Let stand 10 minutes before slicing. Pour off excess fat. Slice and serve with Sauce. Makes 6 to 8 servings.

Meat Loaf 72 Market Street (continued)

SAUCE

4 shallots
2 tablespoons butter
1 sprig thyme
1 bay leaf
Dash crushed black pepper
1 cup dry white wine
1 cup veal or beef stock
1 cup chicken stock
Salt, pepper

Sauté shallots in 1 tablespoon butter with thyme, bay leaf and black pepper. Add white wine and stocks. Season to taste with salt and pepper. Simmer until reduced by half and sauce thickens slightly. Stir in remaining 1 tablespoon butter until melted.

❖

PLUM TREE ORANGE BEEF

Everyone wanted orange beef the way it was made at the Plum Tree in Los Angeles. The trick is using pieces of dried orange peel, found at any Asian market, to flavor the sauce.

1 pound top sirloin steak
¼ teaspoon salt
Oil
Flour Mixture
5 small hot dried chiles
5 pieces dried orange peel
4 pieces ginger root
4 green onions, chopped
Sauce

Cut beef across grain into strips ¾-inch wide and 1½-inches long. Rub beef with salt. Blend 3 tablespoons oil with Flour Mixture. Coat beef strips.

Heat 6 cups oil in large wok or skillet to 320 degrees. Drop beef, piece by piece into oil. Fry until golden brown, about 5 minutes. Remove beef from skillet and drain excess oil. Add 2 tablespoons oil and heat. Add chile peppers, orange peel, ginger root and green onions. Sauté 30 seconds. Add Sauce, stirring constantly, until sauce thickens and boils. Return beef to skillet. Stir-fry until beef is coated evenly with sauce. Makes 4 to 6 servings.

FLOUR MIXTURE

3 tablespoons cornstarch
3 tablespoons flour
¼ cup water
1 egg

Combine cornstarch, flour, water and egg. Mix well.

SAUCE

6 tablespoons vinegar
6 tablespoons sugar
½ cup chicken broth
2 teaspoons cornstarch

Combine vinegar, sugar, chicken broth and cornstarch. Mix well.

❖

PEPPERED ROAST BEEF

This roast cooks at 500 degrees for 5 minutes per pound, then the oven is turned off and the roast is left in the oven for 2 hours to finish cooking with retained oven heat. The result is rare beef, perfectly done.

1 (5- to 6-pound) eye-of-round beef roast
Cracked black pepper, red pepper or combination black and red pepper

Cover roast completely with cracked pepper. Place in roasting pan and roast at 500 degrees 5 minutes per pound. Turn off oven but do not open oven door. Leave roast in oven 2 hours. Remove from oven immediately and let cool. Slice thinly and serve. Makes 10 to 12 servings.

❖

MARILYN LEWIS' PARTY BRISKET

Marilyn Lewis, the creator of the Hamburger Hamlet chains and other restaurants, says this dish goes back to her young family days. "My husband and children did not care for brisket, so I decided to sweeten it up with catsup and use coffee to mellow out the flavor, as you would in chili. It's been a hit ever since."

1 (5- to 6-pound) beef brisket
Water
2 large onions
2 teaspoons salt
2 teaspoons celery salt
Pungent Sauce
Brisket Broth

Place brisket in roasting pan or Dutch oven and add water to cover. Peel onions, score at top and add to pan. Add salt and celery salt. Bring to full boil then skim top. Reduce heat, cover and simmer 3 hours (if using roasting pan, cook over 2 burners).

Remove meat, drain (reserving liquid for broth) and cool. Brush with Pungent Sauce. Cover and let stand overnight.

To serve, slice desired amount of brisket, cutting across grain. Lay slices in Dutch oven and add 1 cup Brisket Broth. Cover and bake at 275 degrees 1 hour. Makes about 10 servings.

PUNGENT SAUCE

2 dashes bottled onion juice
1 dash bottled garlic juice
1 teaspoon coarse black pepper
1 teaspoon instant coffee powder
2 tablespoons brown sugar
2 tablespoons Worcestershire sauce
½ cup catsup

Combine onion and garlic juices, pepper, coffee, sugar, Worcestershire and catsup. Mix well. Makes about ¾ cup.

BRISKET BROTH

Broth from cooked brisket
1 bunch carrots, cut diagonally in large chunks
1 bunch celery, including leaves, cut diagonally in large slices
2 to 3 tablespoons chopped parsley
1 leek, white part only, sliced
5 bouillon cubes
1 cup water

Let broth stand overnight in refrigerator. Skim off fat and discard. Place broth in large pot. Add carrots and celery, parsley and leek.

Dissolve bouillon cubes in water and add to broth. Cover and simmer over low heat 1 hour. Use 1 cup broth to reheat brisket slices. Serve remainder with vegetables or strain and serve vegetables separately. Strained broth may be used as basis for other soups.

❖

GORKY'S STUFFED CABBAGE

Readers have enjoyed this Russian dish from the former Gorky's in Los Angeles. It reminds many of grandma's cooking.

1 large or 2 medium cabbages
1 ½ pounds ground beef
2 cups cooked rice
2 eggs, lightly beaten
1 cup chopped onion
1 cup grated carrots
1 teaspoon salt
¼ teaspoon black pepper
Sweet-Sour Sauce

Cook cabbage in water to halfway cover cabbage until tender but not soft, about 30 to 40 minutes, depending on size of cabbage. Cool, core and carefully separate leaves.

Combine beef, rice, eggs, onion, carrots, salt and pepper. Mix well. Roll filling into 8 balls. Place each ball on lower third of large cabbage leaf. Tuck in sides and bottom of cabbage and place, seam-side down, in baking dish.

Pour Sweet-Sour Sauce over cabbage rolls. Cover with foil and bake at 350 degrees 30 minutes. Uncover and bake 10 minutes longer or until lightly browned. Makes 8 rolls.

SWEET-SOUR SAUCE

2 (8-ounce) cans tomato sauce
1 ½ cups water
1 cup brown sugar, packed, or to taste
¾ cup apple cider vinegar

Combine tomato sauce, water, brown sugar and vinegar in saucepan. Bring to boil, reduce heat and simmer 10 minutes or until slightly thickened.

❖

SALISBURY STEAK

A comforting beef dish that eludes many contemporary cookbooks.

> *1 pound ground beef*
> *1 teaspoon salt*
> *$\frac{1}{8}$ teaspoon black pepper*
> *Mushroom Sauce*

Combine beef, salt and pepper in bowl and mix well. Shape into 2 flat oval patties for large steaks or 4 oval patties for medium. Pan-fry over medium-high heat 5 to 6 minutes on each side for rare, 7 minutes for medium, 8 to 9 minutes for well done. Reserve pan drippings, if desired, for Mushroom Sauce. Serve topped with Mushroom Sauce. Makes 2 large or 4 medium servings.

Note: For seasoned patties mix ground beef with minced onion, celery, parsley and any dried or fresh herb, as desired.

> **MUSHROOM SAUCE**
>
> *2 tablespoons butter*
> *$\frac{1}{2}$ pound mushrooms, thinly sliced*
> *1 medium onion, minced*
> *$\frac{1}{4}$ cup roasting-pan drippings or 2 tablespoons beef glaze or granules*
> *$\frac{1}{4}$ cup flour*
> *2 cups beef broth*
> *Salt, pepper*

Melt butter in skillet. Add mushrooms and onion and sauté until onion is tender. Stir in pan drippings. Mix in flour until well blended. Gradually stir in broth. Bring to boil, stirring constantly until thickened. Season to taste with salt and pepper.

❖

SOFT TACOS

We've used pork as the main ingredient in these flavorful tacos but you can use cooked chicken or beef or prepare without any meat.

6 to 12 corn tortillas
Guacamole
Cooked roast pork, diced or shredded, heated
Canned refried beans, heated
Chopped onions or green onions
Cilantro sprigs
Diced tomatoes
Shredded Cheddar cheese
Bottled or canned chile salsa
Sour cream, optional

Heat tortillas on lightly greased griddle or skillet until pliable. Place hot tortillas in napkin-lined basket or other container. Place guacamole, meat and refried beans in serving dishes next to tortillas. Arrange onions, cilantro, tomatoes, cheese, salsa and sour cream in separate bowls. Spread guacamole on tortillas first, then add meat and beans. Top with condiments, as desired, and fold tortilla around contents. Makes 6 servings.

GUACAMOLE

1 ripe avocado
Dash lemon juice
1 tomato, peeled and chopped
1 small onion, minced
1 small clove garlic, minced
Dash salt
Dash chile powder

Mash avocado with lemon juice in small bowl. Add tomato, onion, garlic, salt and chile powder. Chill. Makes about $1\frac{1}{4}$ cups.

❖

STICKY BEEF BONES

Readers just love these Sticky Beef Bones. You can use pork ribs instead.

1 cup vinegar
½ cup honey
2 tablespoons Worcestershire sauce
½ cup catsup
1 teaspoon salt
1 teaspoon dry mustard
1 teaspoon paprika
¼ teaspoon black pepper
1 clove garlic, minced
4 pounds beef ribs

Combine vinegar, honey, Worcestershire, catsup, salt, mustard, paprika, pepper and garlic in saucepan. Cover, bring to boil, reduce heat and simmer 15 minutes.

Place ribs in single layer in baking pan. Cover with hot marinade and let stand 1 hour. Drain off marinade, then bake ribs at 325 degrees 1 hour, turning and basting often with marinade. Makes 6 servings.

❖

HONEY HAM

Laura Wang, a reader, shared her recipe for homemade honey-baked ham which is similar to the spiral sliced ham sold in stores.

1 (about 7-pound) medium smoked pork picnic shoulder
2 cups sugar
1 cup honey or brown sugar, packed
1 (6-ounce) can frozen orange juice, thawed
1 teaspoon whole cloves

Make crosswise slits, ½-inch apart, halfway through pork to where knife touches bone. Place in deep bowl and barely cover with water. Stir in sugar. Soak at least 2 days in refrigerator.

Drain. Place pork in roasting pan lined with enough foil to wrap completely. Pour honey and orange juice all over pork. Stud cloves all over meat. Wrap tightly with

Honey Ham (continued)

foil. Bake at 200 degrees 6 to 7 hours, unwrapping and basting occasionally with honey mixture.

Unwrap and bake at 450 degrees about 15 minutes for slightly crisp skin. Makes about 8 servings.

❖

CHINESE SPARERIBS

This basic Chinese marinade flavors and tenderizes the ribs.

4 to 5 pounds spareribs
Water
¼ cup honey
¼ cup soy sauce
¼ cup sherry
¼ cup wine vinegar
1 clove garlic, crushed
⅛ teaspoon powdered ginger
Sesame seeds

Simmer ribs in water to cover, 40 minutes. Drain.

Mix honey, soy sauce, sherry, vinegar, garlic and ginger and simmer 10 minutes.

Place ribs on grill over moderately hot coals. Brush with sauce while grilling on both sides until golden brown. Or weave ribs on spit and cook until glazed and brown, basting frequently with sauce. Cut between ribs. Roll ribs in sesame seeds to coat. Makes 4 to 6 servings.

❖

VEGETABLE DISHES

When we sat down to collect the best and the most frequently requested vegetable dishes, we were amazed at the number we could not do without. There are recipes here that will strengthen and enrich any vegetarian's recipe file, such as Mrs. Gooch's Natural Foods Market burgers made with soy beans and corn, or chili made only with vegetables. But there are vegetable dishes that anyone–vegetarian or not–will want to add to their meals.

❖

Dear S.O.S.:
        I had a recipe for Indian curried vegetables and threw it out in error. It was a delicious recipe and I would appreciate having it again.
–Margaret

Dear Margaret:
        The recipe is from the Bombay Palace restaurant in Los Angeles.

LIKE LOVE'S BEANS

Love's Barbecue restaurant in Los Angeles serves wonderfully satisfying barbecued baked beans but could not share their trade secret for making them. This recipe is considered by many to be very close.

> *1 ½ pounds dried small white beans*
> *2 tablespoons molasses*
> *½ cup brown sugar, packed*
> *Salt, pepper*
> *1 onion, chopped*
> *½ teaspoon dry mustard*
> *¼ pound salt pork, cut into pieces*
> *¼ cup catsup*
> *¼ teaspoon liquid smoke or hickory seasoning*
> *Boiling water*

Cover beans with water and soak overnight. Drain and cover with fresh cold water. Bring to boil, reduce heat and cook 1 hour. Add molasses, brown sugar, salt and pepper to taste, onion, mustard, salt pork, catsup and liquid smoke. Cover and bake at 350 degrees 7 hours. Stir occasionally and add water as necessary to keep beans covered. Makes 8 to 10 servings.

❖

SANTA MARIA BEANS

Rodeo week in Santa Maria, California, prompted requests for ranchero-style beans. Serve with Santa Maria barbecued beef, the recipe is included in the meat chapter.

> *1 pound small pink beans (pinkitas or pintos)*
> *1 slice bacon, diced*
> *¼ cup diced ham*
> *1 small clove garlic, minced*
> *¾ cup tomato purée*
> *¼ cup canned red chile sauce*
> *1 tablespoon sugar*
> *1 teaspoon dry mustard*
> *1 teaspoon salt*

Cover beans with water and soak overnight. Drain and cover with fresh cold water and simmer 2 hours or until tender. Meanwhile, sauté bacon and ham until lightly browned. Add garlic and sauté 1 to 2 minutes, then add tomato purée, chile sauce, sugar, mustard and salt.

Drain most of liquid off beans and stir in sauce. Keep warm over very low heat or in low oven until ready to serve. Makes 6 to 8 servings.

❖

SILLY CARROTS

We can't count the number of requests for this unusual carrot recipe made with tomato soup from a "My Best Recipe" winner in 1981.

2 pounds carrots, peeled and sliced
1 (10-ounce) can tomato soup
¾ cup sugar
¾ cup wine vinegar
¼ cup oil
1 teaspoon prepared mustard
1 large onion, diced
1 medium green pepper, diced
4 stalks celery, diced
Salt, pepper

Cook carrots in boiling water just until tender. Drain and set aside. Combine tomato soup, sugar, vinegar, oil, mustard, onion, green pepper and celery and season to taste with salt and pepper. Heat and stir to boiling. Reduce heat and simmer 10 minutes. Pour over drained carrots. Serve hot or refrigerate for salad. Makes 6 to 8 servings.

❖

GULLIVER'S CREAMED SPINACH

Popularity of this soufflé-like spinach side dish from Gulliver's restaurant in Los Angeles hasn't waned since the recipe was first obtained in 1974. Readers also enjoy Gulliver's creamed corn, the recipe follows.

2 (10-ounce) packages frozen leaf spinach
3 slices bacon
1 small onion
3 tablespoons flour
1 ¼ cups milk
1 teaspoon salt
½ teaspoon coarsely ground black pepper

Thaw spinach, squeeze completely dry. Chop spinach, bacon and onion very fine. In saucepan, sauté bacon with onion until bacon is cooked.

Stir in flour to make smooth paste. Gradually add milk. Bring to boil and simmer 10 minutes over low heat until thickened. Add salt and pepper. Add spinach to cream sauce and mix to blend. Heat through. Makes 6 servings.

❖

GULLIVER'S CREAMED CORN

8 ears corn
1 cup whipping cream
2 teaspoons salt
1 teaspoon sugar
Butter or margarine
2 teaspoons flour
Grated Parmesan cheese

Cut corn from cob and place in saucepan with whipping cream. Bring to boil, reduce heat and simmer 5 minutes. Stir in salt and sugar. Melt 2 teaspoons butter in small pan and stir in flour. Do not brown. Stir butter-flour roux into corn and cook until slightly thickened. Turn corn into oven-proof dish. Sprinkle with cheese and dot with butter. Brown under broiler. Makes 8 to 10 servings.

SPICY CHINESE EGGPLANT

Readers often request this spicy eggplant dish common in many Sichuan or Mandarin restaurants in Southern California.

3 tablespoons black Chinkiang vinegar or balsamic vinegar

2 teaspoons sugar

Salt

1 ¼ pounds Japanese eggplants

⅓ cup olive oil

½ teaspoon crushed hot red pepper, or to taste

2 tablespoons minced parsley

Mix vinegar, sugar and ¾ teaspoon salt. Cut eggplants into ½-inch-wide, 2-inch-long strips.

Heat olive oil in wok or large skillet over medium-high heat. Add eggplants and cook, stirring constantly, until lightly browned, about 5 minutes. Cook in 2 batches, if necessary. Add red pepper and stir briefly. Remove pan from heat and add vinegar mixture. Stir until liquid is thoroughly absorbed, 1 to 2 minutes. Stir in parsley. Makes 4 servings.

❖

SPINACH LOAF SUPREME

This old-time dish performs well as a meatless main dish for anyone looking for good, low-cost nutrition.

1 ¼ cups cooked or canned chopped spinach

1 cup bread crumbs

1 cup shredded Cheddar cheese

1 egg, well beaten

1 teaspoon seasoned salt

Dash pepper

1 tablespoon lemon juice

Quick Tomato Sauce

Combine spinach with bread crumbs, cheese, egg, salt, pepper and lemon juice, mixing well. Turn into buttered shallow baking pan or loaf pan and bake at 350

Spinach Loaf Supreme (continued)

degrees 25 to 30 minutes or until set. Serve with Quick Tomato Sauce. Makes 6 servings.

QUICK TOMATO SAUCE

2 tablespoons butter or margarine
2 tablespoons flour
½ teaspoon salt
Dash pepper
1 teaspoon onion juice
1 cup milk
¾ cup catsup

Melt butter in saucepan and add flour. Cook and stir until well blended. Add salt, pepper, onion juice and milk and cook and stir until thick. Add catsup gradually, stirring constantly until heated through.

❖

TONY AWARD ONION LOAF

Because we were unable to extract a recipe for the wonderful onion loaf served at Tony Roma's chain restaurants for our readers, we developed our own with a tip from the restaurant: Pack the loaf lightly.

4 to 6 mild white onions
1 cup milk
3 eggs, beaten
Salt
2 cups pancake mix, about
Oil for deep frying
Parsley sprigs

Slice onions crosswise and separate into rings. Soak rings in mixture of milk, eggs and salt to taste in bowl 30 minutes.

Dip each onion ring in pancake mix and fry in oil heated to 375 degrees until golden brown. Pack fried onions loosely, without pressing, into 8 x 4-inch loaf pan and bake at 400 degrees 10 to 15 minutes. Turn out onto serving plate. Garnish with parsley. Makes 4 to 6 servings.

SPECIAL SWEET POTATO CASSEROLE

Readers rave about this casserole. We think it's the crunchy topping made with nuts, coconut and brown sugar that makes the difference.

4 cups hot mashed sweet potatoes
Butter or margarine
2 tablespoons sugar
2 eggs, beaten
½ cup milk
⅓ cup chopped pecans
⅓ cup flake coconut
⅓ cup brown sugar, packed
2 tablespoons flour

Mix sweet potatoes, ⅓ cup butter and sugar. Beat in eggs and milk. Pour mixture into 1½- to 2-quart casserole. Combine pecans, coconut, brown sugar and flour. Stir in 2 tablespoons melted butter. Sprinkle mixture over sweet potatoes. Bake at 325 degrees 1 hour. Makes 6 to 8 servings.

❖

YAM AND APPLE CASSEROLE

It's a great choice at Thanksgiving or whenever serving turkey or pork roast.

4 medium (about 1 ¾ pounds) yams
Boiling water
2 medium Golden Delicious apples
¼ cup butter or margarine, cut in thin pats
¼ cup dark brown sugar, packed
½ teaspoon ground mace

Scrub yams under cold running water. Place in medium saucepan and cover with boiling water. Cover pan and boil until almost tender, about 25 minutes. Cool slightly and remove skins. Cut in ½-inch-thick crosswise slices.

Peel and core apples. Cut each in 6 rings.

Layer yams and apples in 1½-quart buttered casserole. Dot with butter and sprinkle with brown sugar and mace. Bake, covered, at 350 degrees until apples are very tender, about 1 hour. Makes 4 to 6 servings.

LAWRY'S SOUR CREAM TORTILLA CASSEROLE

Lawry's California Center served this inexpensive but filling side dish casserole before closing its doors.

1 ¼ cups chopped onion

Oil

1 (1-pound, 12-ounce) can tomatoes

1 (1 ½-ounce) package taco seasoning mix

2 tablespoons chile salsa

12 corn tortillas

1 pound Jack cheese, shredded

2 cups sour cream

1 teaspoon seasoned salt

Seasoned pepper

Sauté ½ cup onion in 2 tablespoons oil until tender. Add tomatoes, seasoning mix and chile salsa. Simmer 15 to 20 minutes. Set aside to cool.

Fry tortillas lightly in small amount of oil, 10 to 15 seconds on each side, just until soft. Pour ½ cup sauce in bottom of 13 x 9-inch baking dish. Arrange layer of tortillas over sauce (tortillas can overlap). Top with ⅓ of sauce, ⅓ of remaining onions and a ⅓ cheese. Repeat layering procedure twice. Combine sour cream and seasoned salt, spread over cheese to edges of dish. Sprinkle lightly with seasoned pepper and bake at 325 degrees 25 to 30 minutes. To serve, cut into squares. Makes 10 to 12 servings.

❖

EL CHOLO GREEN CORN TAMALES

Tamales, like this recipe from the El Cholo restaurant chain, are traditionally served during the holiday season in many Southern California homes.

12 ears yellow corn
¼ pound cornmeal
¼ cup shortening
¼ cup butter
¼ cup sugar
¼ cup half and half or whipping cream
Salt
12 (1-ounce) Cheddar cheese strips, halved
1 (12-ounce) can green chiles, cut into strips

Cut both ends from ears of corn. Remove husks, reserving for wrapping. Cut corn kernels off cobs. Grind kernels with cornmeal in food processor. Set aside.

Beat shortening and butter until creamy. Add sugar, half and half and season to taste with salt. Add corn mixture and mix well.

For each tamale, overlap 2 corn husks lengthwise. Spread ¼-cup layer of corn mixture onto husks to within 1 inch of edges. Place 1 cheese strip and 1 chili strip over filling. Top with 2 tablespoons corn mixture. Fold edges of corn husks over filling to cover completely.

Place husks on square of parchment paper. Fold ends of corn husks, then fold sides of parchment over tamale and fold up ends. Tie string around ends to hold in place. Continue until all tamales are prepared.

Place tamales on steamer rack and steam 1 inch over simmering water about 35 to 45 minutes. Makes 24 tamales.

❖

EL TORITO'S SWEET CORN CAKES

El Torito restaurant serves this popular casserole as a side dish with grilled chicken or meat.

2 tablespoons lard
¼ cup butter
½ cup masa
3 tablespoons cold water
10 ounces frozen corn kernels or 2 large ears corn, kernels removed
3 tablespoons cornmeal
¼ cup sugar
2 tablespoons whipping cream
¼ teaspoon baking powder
¼ teaspoon salt

Place lard and butter in mixer bowl and whip until butter softens. Continue whipping until mixture becomes fluffy and creamy. Add masa gradually and mix until thoroughly incorporated. Add water gradually, mixing thoroughly.

Place corn kernels in blender and blend until coarsely chopped. Stir into masa mixture.

Place cornmeal, sugar, whipping cream, baking powder and salt in large mixing bowl. Mix quickly. Add butter-masa mixture. Mix just until blended.

Pour into buttered 8-inch square baking pan. Cover with foil and bake at 350 degrees 40 to 50 minutes or until corn cake has firm texture. Allow to stand at room temperature 15 minutes before cutting. Cut into squares or use small ice cream scoop to portion servings. Makes about 10 servings.

❖

Follow Your Heart Nut Burger

Sources at the Follow Your Heart restaurants, located in Santa Barbara and Canoga Park, claim that their nut burgers have been one of the most popular items on their vegetarian menu. These soft, nutty burgers contain no binding and require careful handling. Because the mixture is already cooked, only browning on the griddle is necessary.

1/2 cup raw sunflower seeds
1/2 cup raw almonds
1/3 cup raw walnuts
1/2 cup raw cashews
1/2 cup chopped onion
2 tablespoons chopped green pepper
1/2 cup chopped yellow squash
2 tablespoons soy sauce
1/2 cup water
1 clove garlic, minced or pressed
Dash dried basil
Dash dried dill weed
1/2 cup chopped or shredded carrots
1/2 cup bulgur (cracked wheat)
8 slices Cheddar cheese
8 sesame seed buns
8 tablespoons Thousand Island dressing
8 tomato slices
2 cups alfalfa sprouts

Grind sunflower seeds, almonds, walnuts and cashews in blender, food processor or nut mill until coarsely ground. Set aside.

Combine onion, green pepper and squash. Mix soy sauce and water in small bowl. Process vegetables with garlic, basil and dill weed, adding soy mixture a little at a time in blender.

Pour purée into saucepan and place over medium-high heat. Add carrots and bulger, bring to boil, stirring often. Reduce heat and simmer 10 minutes.

Remove from heat and add nuts. Mix well. Form into 8 patties or scoop into 8 (2 1/2-ounce) portions onto baking sheet and flatten slightly. Refrigerate until ready to use.

Bake or grill until heated through and browned on 1 side. Do not turn. Top each patty with slice of cheese and melt slightly.

Serve patties in sesame buns. Top each with 1 tablespoon Thousand Island dress-

Follow Your Heart Nut Burger (continued)

ing, tomato slice and ¼ cup alfalfa sprouts. Makes 8 servings.

Note: Scoop of nut burger mixture can be placed directly on one side of split bun with or without cheese slice and baked or broiled until heated through or toasted. Then dress as directed.

❖

GOOCHBURGERS

Mrs. Gooch's Natural Foods Market in Glendale, California, developed this burger using lecithin, one of several phosphatides (found in egg yolk, soy beans and corn), and powdered kelp, a seaweed available in any health food store. The burgers may sound clinical, but they are incredibly healthful and tasty.

> *1 cup bulgur wheat*
> *1 cup hot water*
> *1 onion, finely diced*
> *4 cloves garlic, pressed, or 1 tablespoon dried flakes*
> *Oil*
> *½ teaspoon dried thyme*
> *½ teaspoon dried oregano*
> *2 teaspoons dried celery flakes, finely ground*
> *2 tablespoons dried mushrooms, finely ground*
> *1 cup rolled oats, finely ground*
> *1 tablespoon lecithin granules*
> *½ cup ground almonds*
> *½ cup ground toasted hazelnuts*
> *1 teaspoon kelp powder, optional*
> *1 teaspoon salt*
> *1 teaspoon black pepper*
> *Vegetable stock or water*

In large bowl, soak bulgur in hot water 30 minutes.

Meanwhile, in skillet sauté onion and garlic in1 tablespoon oil, 10 minutes.

To soaked bulgur, add thyme, oregano, celery flakes, mushrooms, oats, lecithin, almonds, hazelnuts, kelp, salt and pepper. Add onion mixture and mix well. Add vegetable stock, 2 tablespoons at time, as needed to moisten. Let stand 20 minutes. Adjust seasonings to taste.

Form into patties. Gently fry patties in hot oil until browned on both sides, or bake at 350 degrees 10 to 15 minutes until browned and done. Makes 7 patties.

GELSON'S VEGETABLE CHILI

Gelson's grocery stores in Southern California created this recipe for a vegetable chili that readers adore.

½ cup dry kidney beans
Water
¼ cup bulgur
½ cup olive oil
1 small red onion, cubed
1 small sweet white onion, cubed
1 ½ tablespoons minced garlic
½ cup cubed celery
½ cup cubed carrots
2 tablespoons chile powder
2 tablespoons ground cumin
½ teaspoon cayenne pepper
4 teaspoons chopped fresh basil
1 tablespoon chopped fresh oregano
1 yellow squash, cubed
1 zucchini, cubed
1 green pepper, cubed
1 red pepper, cubed
1 cup mushrooms
½ cup cubed tomatoes
½ cup tomato paste
¾ cup white wine
Salt, pepper

Soak beans in cold water to cover overnight. Drain off water. Add 3 cups fresh water to beans and cook over medium heat until tender, about 45 minutes. Set aside.

Bring ½ cup water to boil. Pour over bulgur in bowl. Let stand 30 minutes to soften wheat (water will be absorbed).

Heat olive oil in large saucepan. Add red and sweet onions. Sauté until tender. Add garlic, celery and carrots. Sauté until glazed. Add chile powder, cumin, cayenne, basil and oregano. Cook over low heat until carrots are almost tender. Add squash, zucchini, green and red peppers and mushrooms. Cook 4 minutes. Add bulgur, tomatoes and beans with liquid. Cook 30 minutes or until vegetables are tender. Mix tomato paste with white wine until smooth. Stir into vegetable mixture. Season to taste with salt and pepper. Makes 8 servings.

BOMBAY PALACE NINE-VEGETABLE CURRY

The Bombay Palace restaurant in Los Angeles provided this recipe for vegetable curry.

1/4 pound broccoli, cut into florets

1/4 pound green or sweet red pepper, cut into diamonds or small cubes

1/4 pound carrots, peeled, sliced and cut into diamonds or small cubes

1/4 pound cauliflower, cut into florets

1/4 pound green beans, sliced and cut into diamonds or small cubes

1 large potato, peeled, sliced and cut into diamonds or small cubes

Water

2 tablespoons butter

1 large onion, minced

2 cloves garlic, minced

2 tomatoes, chopped

2 tablespoons yogurt

Dry Masala

1/2 cup whipping cream

1/4 pound fresh or 1/2 (10-ounce) package frozen green peas, thawed

1 (4-ounce) can mixed fruit cocktail, drained

1/4 cup raisins

12 blanched almonds, slivered

Separately cook broccoli, green pepper, carrots, cauliflower, green beans and potato in boiling salted water until crisp-tender. Drain, set aside.

Melt butter in skillet. Add onion and garlic. Sauté until onion is transparent. Add tomatoes, yogurt and Dry Masala. Simmer 5 minutes. Add parboiled vegetables and simmer 5 minutes longer, adding 1/4 cup water. Cover and simmer 10 minutes. Stir in whipping cream and peas. Remove few cherry pieces from canned fruit for garnish. Add remaining fruit to sauce. Just before serving, top with raisins and almonds and decorate with cherry pieces. Makes 4 to 6 servings.

DRY MASALA

1/2 teaspoon ground cardamom

1/2 teaspoon ground coriander

1/2 teaspoon ground ginger

1/2 teaspoon chile powder

1/2 teaspoon turmeric

Combine cardamom, coriander, ginger, chile powder and turmeric.

PASTA & RICE

Pasta, the Italian macaroni product, came into its own as an important food during America's fitness craze in the sixties and seventies when "carbohydrate loading" was considered an effective way to increase endurance during aerobic events. The U.S. Surgeon General's Office also added its stamp of approval by recommending an increase in our intake of grain foods in the diet. In Southern California, however, the pasta category includes not only the old standbys, such as macaroni and cheese, and skillet spaghetti, but ethnic noodle dishes, such as *Pad Thai*, and spicy Chinese noodles. Other pasta and rice dishes in this chapter are among the most frequently requested.

❖

Dear S.O.S.:
    I am very fond of the noodle dish called Pad Thai served in Thai restaurants. Do you have such a recipe?
–Sharon

Dear Sharon:
    This recipe is from the House of Chan Dara in Hollywood. You can find the fish sauce, tamarind and noodles at any Asian food market.

BULGAR PILAF

Dried, coarsely ground wheat is known as bulgur, a staple of the Middle Eastern diet used in place of rice. It cooks like rice in water or broth and can be used with many other foods, including vegetables, meat and poultry.

3 tablespoons butter or margarine

2 cups bulgur (cracked wheat)

1 teaspoon salt

3 cups chicken broth or water

2 teaspoons grated lemon peel

Additional broth

Melt butter in heavy saucepan or skillet. Add bulgur wheat and cook 5 minutes, stirring frequently. Add salt and chicken broth. Cover and simmer until liquid is absorbed, about 20 minutes. Stir in lemon peel. For soft pilaf, add ½ to 1 cup additional chicken broth, cooking until liquid is absorbed. Makes 6 servings.

❖

COMPANY RICE

The recipe for this cheese, rice and mushroom casserole won the "My Best Recipe" prize in 1972.

½ cup butter or margarine

1 large onion, minced

¾ cup shredded Cheddar cheese

1 ¾ cups rice

1 (4-ounce) can mushrooms, drained

2 (10 ½-ounce) cans consommé

1 cup sliced almonds

Melt butter in skillet, add onion and sauté until tender, but not browned. Combine onion, cheese, rice, mushrooms, consommé and almonds in 4- to 5-quart casserole. Mix well. Cover and bake at 325 degrees 1 hour. Remove cover and bake 15 minutes longer. Makes about 12 servings.

ACAPULCO-LOS ARCOS MEXICAN RICE

The Acapulco-Los Arcos restaurants in Los Angeles serve Mexican rice which readers like—with tomatoes, spices and onion.

1 large onion
2 cups long grain rice
2 ounces lard or chicken fat
2 cups chicken broth
1 cup tomato juice
1 cup diced tomatoes
1 tablespoon chopped parsley
1 teaspoon minced garlic
Dash ground cumin
1 teaspoon salt
Dash white pepper

Sauté onion and rice in lard until lightly browned, 6 to 10 minutes, stirring constantly. Turn into baking dish or casserole.

In large saucepan, combine chicken broth, tomato juice, tomatoes, parsley, garlic, cumin and salt and pepper. Bring to boil. Add broth mixture to rice mixture. Cover and bake at 350 degrees 20 to 30 minutes or until rice is fluffy. Use fork to fluff rice. Let set 15 minutes before serving. Makes 6 to 8 servings.

❖

VEGETARIAN LASAGNA

Health conscious cooks seeking meatless alternatives to old favorites created recipes like this lasagna made with vegetables.

8 ounces lasagna noodles, cooked and drained

2 onions, chopped

4 cloves garlic, minced

3 tablespoons oil

1 (1-pound) can tomato sauce

2 teaspoons dried oregano

1 teaspoon dried basil

¼ cup chopped parsley

2 teaspoons salt

½ pound mushrooms, sliced

1 (1-pound) can kidney beans, lightly mashed

¾ pound mozzarella cheese, thinly sliced

2 cups ricotta cheese

½ cup grated Parmesan cheese

Rinse noodles in cold water to prevent sticking.

Set aside. Sauté onions and garlic in oil until tender. Stir in tomato sauce, oregano, basil, parsley and salt. Cook and stir about 30 minutes or until sauce has thickened. Stir in mushrooms and beans.

To assemble, place layer of noodles in 9-inch square baking dish. Cover with ⅓ of tomato sauce, then ⅓ each of mozzarella, ricotta and Parmesan cheeses. Repeat layers twice, ending with Parmesan cheese. Bake at 375 degrees 20 minutes. Cut into squares to serve. Makes 8 servings.

❖

PAD THAI

This dish from Thailand was made popular on the West Coast by the growing numbers of Thai restaurants. You'll need to purchase fish sauce, tamarind and rice noodles, all of which are found in most Asian grocery stores.

10 ounces pad thai (vermicelli noodles)
Water
2 tablespoons bottled fish sauce (nam pla)
1 tablespoon sugar
¼ cup tamarind juice
3 tablespoons vinegar
½ teaspoon chopped serrano chile
Oil
2 ounces lean pork, thinly sliced to 1 x 2-inch pieces
2 to 3 medium to large shrimp, shelled and deveined
1 ½ teaspoons dried shrimp
1 tablespoon diced baked soybean cake
1 egg
2 teaspoons crushed peanuts
Bean sprouts
1 green onion, sliced very thin

Soak noodles in water to cover.

Combine fish sauce, sugar, tamarind juice, vinegar and chile in bowl.

Heat 1½ tablespoons oil in medium skillet. Add pork, shrimp, dried shrimp, soybean cake and fish sauce mixture and cook over high heat until pork is browned and well cooked.

Thoroughly drain noodles and add to skillet. Stir just enough to dry slightly. Push noodle mixture to one side of skillet. Add 1 tablespoon oil to skillet and heat. Add egg and scramble until firm. Top egg with noodle mixture, 1 teaspoon crushed peanuts and 1 cup bean sprouts. Serve topped with additional bean sprouts, green onion and remaining teaspoon peanuts. Makes 1 to 2 servings.

❖

GELSON'S SPICY SESAME NOODLES

This oriental noodle dish comes from the deli section of Gelson's Market, a grocery store chain in Los Angeles.

1 pound linguine
Sesame oil
1 bunch green onions, cut in 1-inch diagonals
1 bunch broccoli, trimmed, cut into florets, blanched
¼ pound Chinese pea pods, cut into ½-inch diagonals, blanched
1 pound asparagus, blanched and cut in short lengths
1 sweet red pepper, cut julienne
Dijon-Chile Mayonnaise

Cook linguine al dente in boiling salted water. Drain and sprinkle lightly with sesame oil to prevent sticking. Cool.

Add green onions, broccoli, pea pods, asparagus and sweet red pepper. Toss to mix.

Add Dijon-Chile Mayonnaise and mix thoroughly. Serve cold. Makes 6 to 8 servings.

DIJON-CHILE MAYONNAISE

2 eggs
4 egg yolks
1 tablespoon Dijon mustard
3 cups soy oil
2 tablespoons sesame oil
1 teaspoon chile oil
1 tablespoon rice vinegar
1 tablespoon soy sauce
1 tablespoon grated orange zest

Combine eggs, yolks and Dijon mustard in food processor. Add oils slowly in thin stream while machine is running. Add vinegar, soy sauce and orange zest. Makes 3 cups.

❖

SKILLET SPAGHETTI

The unusual method of cooking spaghetti in its own sauce in a skillet has been adopted by many readers over the years.

1 pound ground beef
½ cup chopped onion
1 clove garlic, minced
2 tablespoons oil
1 (15-ounce) can tomato sauce or enchilada sauce
3 cups hot water
7 ounces spaghetti
1 (1 ½-ounce) package spaghetti seasoning mix

In large skillet over medium-high heat, brown beef, onion and garlic in oil, stirring now and then. Add tomato sauce, water, uncooked spaghetti and seasoning mix. Cover and simmer 30 minutes, or until spaghetti is tender, stirring occasionally. Makes 6 to 8 servings.

❖

SPAGHETTI FACTORY SPAGHETTI MIZITHRA

A spaghetti made famous at the Spaghetti Factory, a family restaurant in Los Angeles, can be made with any hard cheese.

1 pound spaghetti
1 cup butter or margarine
½ pound dry ricotta cheese, kasari or caciocavallo, grated
¼ pound Romano cheese, grated
¼ cup chopped parsley

Cook spaghetti until tender but firm to bite. Drain. Melt butter in large skillet until butter turns brown. Meanwhile, combine cheeses. Place spaghetti on platter. Sprinkle with mixed cheeses, then drizzle with browned butter. Sprinkle with parsley. Makes 6 servings.

❖

RONALD REAGAN'S FAVORITE MACARONI AND CHEESE

This dish circulated during former President Reagan's terms of office and became a non-partisan favorite of readers.

½ pound macaroni

1 teaspoon butter

1 egg, beaten

1 teaspoon salt

1 teaspoon dry mustard

1 tablespoon hot water

1 cup milk

3 cups shredded sharp Chedder cheese

Cook macaroni in boiling salted water until tender then drain. Stir in butter and egg.

Mix salt and mustard with hot water and add milk. Add cheese, reserving some to sprinkle on top.

Turn macaroni mixture into buttered casserole. Add milk mixture. Sprinkle with reserved cheese. Bake at 350 degrees 45 minutes or until custard is set and top is crusty. Makes 6 servings.

❖

CAKES

Cake recipes are by far the most requested by readers. Our readers are fascinated by sweets, particularly chocolate desserts. For decades, requests for old favorites, such as *Harvey Wallbanger Cake* and *Broken Glass*, have brought new fans with every passing year to satisfy nostalgic yearnings or their curiosity. Other requests reflect trends such as the carrot cake from the J. Paul Getty Museum cafeteria. Many top favorites are here.

❖

Dear S.O.S.:
Last year I tasted a wonderful pumpkin cheesecake from your column. I've lost the recipe. Can you help?
–Virginia

Dear Virginia:
It's one of our favorite holiday cheesecakes, too.

ABBY'S FABULOUS CHOCOLATE CAKE

When readers requested the recipe for columnist Abigail Van Buren's chocolate cake mentioned in her column, "Dear Abby" came through.

4 (1-ounce) squares unsweetened chocolate
½ cup plus 1 tablespoon butter or margarine
1 cup water
2 cups sifted cake flour
1 ¼ teaspoons baking soda
1 teaspoon salt
2 eggs
1 cup sour cream
2 cups sugar
1 ½ teaspoons vanilla
Fluffy White Frosting

Combine 3 squares chocolate, butter and water in top of double boiler. Heat chocolate mixture over simmering water until chocolate and butter melt. Remove from heat. Cool.

Sift flour, baking soda and salt into large bowl.

Beat eggs with sour cream until blended in medium bowl. Beat in sugar and vanilla. Stir in cooled chocolate mixture. Beat into flour mixture, half at a time, just until smooth. Batter will be thin.

Pour evenly into 2 greased and floured round 8-inch cake pans. Bake at 350 degrees 40 minutes or until center springs back when lightly pressed with finger. Cool in pans on wire racks. Loosen edges with knife and turn out onto racks. Stack layers, spreading ¼ of Fluffy White Frosting on each. Frost top and sides with remaining Fluffy White Frosting, making deep swirls with spatula.

Melt remaining square chocolate with 1 tablespoon butter in cup set in hot water. Stir until smooth. Drizzle over top of cake, letting mixture drip down sides. Makes about 8 servings.

❖

FLUFFY WHITE FROSTING

2 egg whites
¾ cup sugar
½ teaspoon cream of tartar
Dash salt
2 ½ teaspoons cold water
1 teaspoon vanilla

Combine egg whites, sugar, cream of tartar, salt and water in top of large double boiler. Beat until blended. Place over simmering water. Cook, beating constantly with electric or rotary beater, about 7 minutes, or until mixture stands in firm peaks. Remove from water. Stir in vanilla.

❖

CHOCOLATE MAYONNAISE CAKE

The people at Kraft, Inc. traced a recipe like this to a cookbook dating back to the 1930's, but the original source of the recipe is unknown.

2 cups sifted flour
¼ cup unsweetened cocoa powder
1 teaspoon baking soda
¼ teaspoon salt
1 cup mayonnaise
1 cup sugar
1 cup water

Sift flour with cocoa, baking soda and salt. Cream mayonnaise with sugar, blending well. Add flour mixture and water alternately in 3 additions to creamed mixture.

Turn batter into greased and floured 13 x 9-inch pan and bake at 350 degrees 30 to 35 minutes. Cool and frost as desired. Makes 12 servings.

❖

ACAPULCO PRINCESS' BLACK FOREST CAKE

Black Forest Cake ranks among the most favorite chocolate cake. The Royal Princess cruise line sent us this version.

1/4 cup butter or margarine
Sugar
2 eggs
1/2 cup plus 2 tablespoons milk
1 cup cake flour
1/2 teaspoon salt
2 tablespoons cocoa
1 teaspoon baking powder
1/2 teaspoon baking soda
1 tablespoon water
2 tablespoons kirsch, or cherry liqueur
1/2 cup raspberry preserves
2 (17-ounce) cans dark sweet cherries, drained
3 1/2 to 4 cups sweetened whipped cream
Chocolate flakes

Cream butter and 1/3 cup sugar until light and fluffy. Beat in eggs, then milk. Beat until smooth.

Sift together flour, salt, cocoa, baking powder and baking soda. Fold dry ingredients into egg mixture until blended. Pour into greased and floured 8-inch round cake pan. Bake at 350 degrees 30 minutes. Cool 10 minutes then remove from pan. Cool thoroughly on wire rack.

Slice cake crosswise twice to make 3 layers. Layers will be thin. Mix together 1 tablespoon sugar, water and kirsch, then sprinkle top 2 layers (not bottom) with mixture. Spread all 3 layers with raspberry preserves. Cover each layer with cherries, then spread with whipped cream. Place second and third layers atop bottom layer. Sprinkle top with chocolate flakes. Chill until ready to serve. Makes 6 servings.

KNUDSEN NO-BAKE CHEESECAKE

The Knudsen Dairy company developed this no-bake cheesecake for their promotional recipe book. Readers love it.

2 envelopes unflavored gelatin

Sugar

1/4 teaspoon salt

2 eggs, separated

1 cup milk

1 tablespoon lemon juice

1 teaspoon grated lemon peel

1 teaspoon vanilla

Graham Cracker Crust

1 cup whipping cream

3 cups cottage cheese

Mix gelatin, 3/4 cup sugar and salt in top of double boiler. Add egg yolks and milk. Beat until well blended. Cook in top of double boiler over simmering water, stirring constantly, until gelatin is dissolved. Remove from heat. Stir in lemon juice, peel and vanilla. Refrigerate, stirring occasionally, until mixture mounds slightly when dropped from spoon.

Meanwhile, prepare Graham Cracker Crust, reserving 2 tablespoons crumb mixture. Press remaining crumbs into bottom of well-buttered 9-inch springform pan.

Beat egg whites until frothy. Gradually add 1/4 cup sugar and continue beating until stiff and glossy. Whip cream until stiff. Set both whites and cream aside.

Beat cottage cheese in large bowl with electric mixer on high speed until curds break. Blend in thickened gelatin mixture. Fold in whipped cream, then beaten egg whites.

Turn into crumb-lined pan. Sprinkle with reserved crumbs. Refrigerate about 4 hours or until firm. Makes 8 servings.

GRAHAM CRACKER CRUST

3 tablespoons butter, melted

2 tablespoons sugar

1 cup graham cracker crumbs

1/2 teaspoon ground cinnamon

1/2 teaspoon ground nutmeg

With fingers, combine butter, sugar, crumbs, cinnamon and nutmeg.

LA BELLE HELENE CHOCOLATE CHEESECAKE

The intensity of the chocolate flavor in this cake from the wine country appeals to hard-core chocolate cheesecake lovers. For a more sweet, less bitter flavor, use full cup of sugar.

1 tablespoon of butter

3 ounces unsweetened chocolate

9 ounces semisweet chocolate

4 (3-ounce) packages cream cheese, softened

2 tablespoons vanilla

1 cup whipping cream

6 eggs

½ to 1 cup sugar

Chocolate Wafer Crust

Whipped cream

Melt butter. Add chocolates and melt over gentle heat. Cool slightly. Beat cheese until creamy. Add vanilla and whipping cream. Stir in chocolate mixture. Beat eggs with sugar and slowly beat into chocolate mixture. Turn into Chocolate Wafer Crust and bake at 350 degrees 40 to 45 minutes or until cake puffs slightly in center. Cool and chill thoroughly before unmolding. Serve with whipped cream, if desired. Makes 14 to 16 servings.

CHOCOLATE WAFER CRUST

1 (9-ounce) package chocolate wafers

2 tablespoons melted unsalted butter

Crush wafers. Add melted butter and toss to make a crumbly dough. Press into bottom of 9-inch springform pan, to make even layer.

❖

PUMPKIN CHEESECAKE

An annual favorite.

3 (8-ounce) packages cream cheese, softened
1 cup sugar
4 eggs
1 (1-pound) can pumpkin
2 1/2 teaspoons ground ginger
1 tablespoon ground cinnamon
1/2 teaspoon ground nutmeg
1/4 teaspoon ground cloves
1/3 cup brandy
Graham Cracker Crust

Beat cream cheese and sugar until fluffy. Add eggs, one at a time, beating well after each addition until smooth and creamy. Add pumpkin, ginger, cinnamon, nutmeg, cloves and brandy and mix until well blended. Turn cheese mixture into Graham Cracker Crust. Bake at 325 degrees 50 to 60 minutes, or until well puffed. Turn off heat and let cheesecake cool in oven. Makes 6 to 8 servings.

GRAHAM CRACKER CRUST

1 1/2 cups graham cracker crumbs
1/4 cup sugar
1/2 cup butter or margarine, melted

Combine crumbs, sugar and butter and mix until crumbs are moistened. Place crumb mixture in 10-inch springform pan and press 2 inches evenly up sides of pan and on bottom. Bake at 350 degrees 20 minutes.

❖

MISTO BAKERY FLOURLESS CHOCOLATE CAKE

Flourless chocolate cakes came into their own during the confusion over carbohydrates. Today the cakes are loved for what they are–densely chocolate cakes. Misto Bakery and Café in Torrance, California can take credit for this decadent and delightful version.

2 pounds bittersweet chocolate
1 ¼ cups butter, softened
8 eggs, separated
Dash salt
2 tablespoons granulated sugar
Powdered sugar

Melt chocolate and whisk into butter until blended. Beat egg yolks until pale yellow in color, about 5 minutes. Beat egg whites with salt until frothy. Add granulated sugar and beat 5 seconds. Fold chocolate mixture into yolks, then fold in egg whites, blending lightly but well.

Pour into paper-lined, well-buttered 10-inch round cake pan. Bake at 425 degrees 15 minutes. Cake will be soft. Cool completely before removing from pan. Dust with powdered sugar. Makes 8 to 12 servings.

❖

LIKE MISS GRACE'S LEMON CAKE

We finally developed a puckery lemon cake that closely resembles a popular commercial brand requested by hundreds of readers.

1 (23.7-ounce) package Bundt cake mix
3 eggs
1 ¼ cups water
¼ cup lemon juice
1 tablespoon lemon extract
¼ cup butter or margarine, softened
Lemon Glaze

Blend together packets 1 and 2 of cake mix with eggs, water, lemon juice, lemon extract and butter in large bowl. Stir until moistened. (Reserve packet 3 for Lemon

Glaze.) Beat 2 minutes at medium speed of mixer or highest speed of portable mixer. Pour into greased 12-cup fluted tube pan and bake at 325 degrees 45 to 55 minutes, or until wood pick inserted in center comes out clean. Cool until lukewarm. Turn out onto serving platter. Spoon Lemon Glaze over cake and chill until set. Makes about 12 servings.

LEMON GLAZE

Reserved packet of cake mix, plus powdered sugar to make 1 cup
2 tablespoons lemon juice
1 teaspoon finely grated lemon peel

Sprinkle cake mix mixture slowly into lemon juice and blend until smooth. Stir in lemon peel.

❖

HARVEY WALLBANGER CAKE

This cake mix cake, popularized by food companies promoting their cake mix products, has never ceased to intrigue readers.

1 (18 ¼-ounce) package deluxe yellow cake mix
¾ cup orange juice
¼ cup Galliano liqueur
¼ cup vodka
3 eggs
⅓ cup oil
Powdered sugar

Grease and lightly flour 10-inch Bundt pan. Place cake mix, orange juice, Galliano, vodka, eggs and oil in large mixing bowl. Beat 4 minutes at medium speed. Turn batter into prepared pan and spread evenly.

Bake at 350 degrees 45 to 50 minutes. Cool 25 minutes in pan before removing from pan. Sift powdered sugar over top. Makes 1 (10-inch) cake, about 12 servings.

❖

STRAWBERRY CAKE

A Los Angeles Times reader, Linda Adewale of Los Angeles, won a "My Best Recipe" prize in 1983 for this frequently requested recipe.

3/4 cup shortening

1 1/2 cups sugar

1 1/2 teaspoons vanilla

2 1/4 cups sifted cake flour

1 tablespoon baking powder

1 teaspoon salt

Fresh strawberries

2/3 cup milk

Red food color, optional

5 stiffly beaten egg whites

Creamy Strawberry Frosting

Cream shortening with sugar until light. Add vanilla and mix well. Resift flour with baking powder and salt.

Wash strawberries and remove stems. Mash enough strawberries to measure 1/2 cup purée. Combine purée and milk. Add sifted dry ingredients to creamed mixture alternately with milk mixture. Add red food color to tint pink, if desired.

Gently fold in beaten egg whites. Pour into 2 greased and floured 9-inch layer cake pans and bake at 375 degrees 18 to 20 minutes or until cake tester inserted in center comes out clean. Cool 10 minutes.

Remove from pans and cool completely. Frost with Creamy Strawberry Frosting. Makes 8 to 10 servings.

CREAMY STRAWBERRY FROSTING

Fresh strawberries

2 tablespoons flour

1/3 cup milk

1/2 cup granulated sugar

1/4 cup butter or margarine, softened

1/4 cup shortening

Dash salt

1/2 to 3/4 cup powdered sugar

1 teaspoon vanilla

Red food color, optional

Wash strawberries and remove stems. Mash enough to measure $\frac{1}{4}$ cup strawberry purée. Combine purée with flour and milk in saucepan and cook, stirring, over low heat until thickened. Cool.

Cream granulated sugar with butter and shortening and add to cooled mixture. Beat until nearly doubled in volume. Gradually beat in salt and enough powdered sugar until good spreading consistency. Stir in vanilla and add enough food color to tint pink, if desired. Makes enough frosting for 2 (9-inch) cake layers.

❖

THE NEXT BEST THING TO ROBERT REDFORD CAKE

Perhaps it's the name or the convenient ingredients used to make this popular cake, but the Next Best Thing to Robert Redford Cake continues to be one of the most tantalizing cake recipes for our readers.

1 cup flour
½ cup butter or margarine, softened
1 cup finely chopped pecans
1 (8-ounce) package cream cheese, softened
1 cup sugar
1 (8-ounce) carton frozen non-dairy whipped topping, thawed
1 (6 ¾-ounce) package instant vanilla pudding mix
1 (6 ¾-ounce) package instant chocolate pudding mix
3 cups cold milk
Grated chocolate candy bar, optional

Prepare bottom crust by mixing flour with butter and pecans until crumb-like. Press mixture into greased 13 x 9-inch baking pan. Bake at 350 degrees 15 to 20 minutes until lightly golden. Cool.

Beat cream cheese with sugar until smooth. Fold in half of whipped topping. Spread mixture over cooled crust. Combine vanilla and chocolate pudding mixes. Beat in milk until smooth and thickened. Spread over cream cheese layer.

Spread remaining whipped topping over top. Sprinkle with grated chocolate candy bar. Cover and refrigerate overnight. Makes 16 servings.

❖

J. PAUL GETTY MUSEUM CARROT CAKE

The J. Paul Getty Museum in Malibu produced one of the most popular carrot cakes we have printed.

1 ½ cups corn oil
2 cups sugar
3 eggs
2 cups flour
2 teaspoons ground cinnamon
2 teaspoons baking soda
2 teaspoons vanilla
1 teaspoon salt
2 cups shredded carrots
1 cup chopped walnuts
½ cup crushed pineapple, drained
Cream Cheese Frosting

Combine oil, sugar, eggs, flour, cinnamon, baking soda, vanilla, salt, carrots, walnuts and pineapple in large bowl. Mix until blended. Pour into greased 13 x 9-inch pan and bake at 350 degrees 1 hour. Frost with Cream Cheese Frosting, if desired. Makes about 12 servings.

CREAM CHEESE FROSTING

1 (3-ounce) package cream cheese, softened
1 ¼ cups powdered sugar
½ cup margarine, softened
⅛ cup well-drained crushed pineapple
¼ cup chopped walnuts

Mix cream cheese, powdered sugar and margarine until fluffy. Add pineapple and walnuts. Mix well.

❖

CLIFTON'S ZUCCHINI CAKE

Clifton's Silver Spoon, a cafeteria chain in Los Angeles, offers this zucchini cake, which became famous during the height of the health food movement.

2 cups sugar
1 cup oil
3 eggs
2 cups flour
1 teaspoon baking soda
1 teaspoon salt
1 tablespoon ground cinnamon
2 cups shredded unpeeled zucchini, packed
1 cup finely chopped nuts
1 tablespoon vanilla
Cream Cheese Frosting

Combine sugar, oil and eggs in bowl of electric mixer. Beat at medium speed 4 minutes. Sift flour with baking soda, salt and cinnamon.

Fold zucchini and nuts into sugar mixture. Fold in flour mixture and vanilla, blending thoroughly.

Turn batter into well-greased 9-inch tube pan. Bake at 350 degrees 60 to 65 minutes. Cool in pan on rack 15 minutes or longer. Remove from pan and cool thoroughly on rack before frosting with Cream Cheese Frosting. Makes about 12 servings.

CREAM CHEESE FROSTING

3 cups powdered sugar, sifted
2 (3-ounce) packages cream cheese, softened
5 tablespoons margarine
1 teaspoon lemon extract

Mix or beat powdered sugar with cream cheese, margarine and lemon extract until thoroughly blended.

❖

PINK CHAMPAGNE CAKE

The requests for this champagne cake come during the wedding months of June and July.

2 ¾ cups sifted flour
1 tablespoon baking powder
1 teaspoon salt
⅔ cup shortening
1 ½ cups sugar
¾ cup champagne
6 egg whites
Coconut Filling
Fondant Frosting
6 large marshmallows, quartered

Resift flour with baking powder and salt.

Cream shortening with 1 cup sugar until light and fluffy. Blend in flour mixture and champagne alternately, mixing to smooth batter. Beat egg whites until stiff. Gradually beat in remaining ½ cup sugar, continuing to beat to stiff meringue. Fold about half of meringue into batter, mixing gently but thoroughly with whisk. Gently fold in remaining meringue. Turn into 2 greased and floured 9-inch cake pans. Bake at 350 degrees 25 to 30 minutes, just until cake tests done. Let stand 10 minutes, then turn out onto wire racks to cool.

When layers are cool, fill with Coconut Filling between layers. Using ⅔ cup Fondant Frosting, spread thin layer smoothly over top and sides. This seals any crumbs. Pour about ½ cup additional frosting over top of cake and spread quickly to smooth layer. Cover sides of cake with second layer of frosting. Dip marshmallow quarters in remaining frosting to coat both sides and set randomly over top and sides of cake. Makes 10 to 12 servings.

COCONUT FILLING

¼ cup butter or margarine
16 large marshmallows, quartered
1 tablespoon white wine
1 cup flake coconut

Combine butter, marshmallows and wine in top of double boiler. Set over simmering water and stir occasionally until marshmallows are melted. Remove from heat and stir in coconut. Cool until thick enough to spread.

FONDANT FROSTING

1 pound powdered sugar
¼ cup light corn syrup
¼ cup water
1 ½ teaspoons vanilla
Dash salt
Few drops almond extract
2 to 3 drops red food color, optional

Sift sugar into top of double boiler. Add corn syrup and water. Stir over simmering water until smooth. Blend in vanilla, salt and almond extract. Stir in food color, if desired. Keep frosting warm while using so it spreads smoothly.

❖

BROKEN GLASS CAKE

This unique cake goes back to the days when fruit-flavored gelatin products first came on the market. The multi-colored gelatin squares make this an especially festive cake, another wedding favorite.

1 (3-ounce) package orange-flavored gelatin

1 (3-ounce) package cherry-flavored gelatin

1 (3-ounce) package lime-flavored gelatin

3 cups boiling water

2 cups cold water

1 cup pineapple juice

1/4 cup sugar

1 (3-ounce) package lemon-flavored gelatin

1 1/2 cups graham cracker crumbs

1/3 cup melted butter or margarine

2 cups whipping cream

Prepare orange, cherry and lime gelatins separately, using 1 cup boiling water and 1/2 cup cold water for each. Pour each flavor into 8-inch square pan and chill until firm.

Mix pineapple juice and sugar and heat until sugar is dissolved. Remove from heat. Dissolve lemon gelatin in hot juice, then add 1/2 cup cold water. Chill until slightly thickened.

Combine graham cracker crumbs and butter and press onto bottom of 9-inch springform pan.

Cut firm orange, cherry and lime gelatins into 1/2-inch cubes.

Whip cream until stiff and blend with lemon gelatin mixture. Fold in gelatin cubes. Pour into crumb-lined pan. Chill at least 5 hours.

Run thin knife or spatula around sides of pan and remove sides of pan before serving. Makes 16 servings.

❖

COOKIES

There is not a cookie in this chapter that has not been printed several times. These are the most popular cookie recipes in our file. And they range in concept, flavors and styles to suit many divergent tastes, from the sophisticated biscotti to the nostalgic chocolate chip cookies served for years in the Los Angeles School Cafeterias, and hermits which date back to the thirties.

❖

Dear S.O.S.:
    My grandchildren love the oatmeal raisin cookies at Disneyland. Do you suppose you can obtain the recipe?
–Mrs. T.C.

Dear Mrs. T.C.:
    Mickey Mouse was happy, indeed, to spell out the recipe.

SOFT CHOCOLATE CHIP COOKIES

Mrs. Field's has always denied any association with this cookie thought by many who either purchased or circulated the recipe to be from her kitchen. However, the circulating cookie is surprisingly similar in texture and taste.

1 cup butter, softened

1 cup granulated sugar

1 cup brown sugar, packed

2 eggs

1 teaspoon vanilla

2 cups flour

2 ½ cups oats

½ teaspoon salt

1 teaspoon baking powder

1 teaspoon baking soda

1 (12-ounce) package semisweet chocolate chips

1 (4-ounce) bar milk chocolate, grated

1 ½ cups chopped nuts

Cream butter with sugars in mixer bowl. Add eggs and vanilla, beating well.

Mix flour, oats, salt, baking powder and baking soda in another bowl. Place small amounts in blender and process until mixture turns to powder. Mix butter-egg mixture with flour mixture just until blended. Add chocolate pieces, milk chocolate and chopped nuts. Roll into balls about size of golf ball and place 2 inches apart on ungreased baking sheet. Bake at 375 degrees 12 minutes. Makes 3 to 4 dozen cookies.

❖

CITY SCHOOL FLYING SAUCERS

Huge cookies, the size of saucers, served for years at Los Angeles City Schools have become a Food Section favorite.

1 (6-ounce) package semisweet chocolate pieces
1 ½ cups sifted flour
1 teaspoon salt
½ teaspoon baking soda
¾ cup shortening
1 ½ cups brown sugar, packed
1 egg
1 teaspoon vanilla
¼ cup milk
½ cup oats
1 cup raisins
1 cup diced almonds

Melt chocolate in top of double boiler over hot water. Sift flour with salt and baking soda.

Cream shortening with sugar, egg and vanilla until light and fluffy. Mix in chocolate and flour mixture thoroughly. Stir in milk, oats and raisins. Chill.

Shape into balls about ¾-inch diameter and roll in almonds. Place on greased baking sheets about 3 inches apart and flatten with bottom of glass. Bake at 375 degrees 10 minutes. Makes about 1½ dozen.

❖

DISNEYLAND'S OATMEAL-RAISIN COOKIES

Disneyland is often a source of baked recipes requested by readers who visit the many restaurants in the amusement park.

3 ¼ cups flour

1 tablespoon baking powder

1 ½ teaspoons ground cinnamon

1 teaspoon salt

1 teaspoon baking soda

2 cups plus 2 tablespoons shortening

1 ¾ cups brown sugar, packed

1 ½ cups granulated sugar

3 eggs

1 teaspoon vanilla

4 cups oats

2 ½ cups raisins

Blend flour, baking powder, cinnamon, salt and baking soda in mixing bowl. Set aside.

Blend shortening, brown sugar, granulated sugar, eggs and vanilla in mixing bowl until fluffy. Mix in dry ingredients until well blended, about 2 minutes. Stir in oats and raisins.

Place No. 24 scoop size balls or 2½ tablespoons dough on baking sheet and press down until about ¼-inch thick and about 3-inches across. Bake at 350 degrees 9 to 12 minutes. Cool on baking sheet. Makes about 2 dozen.

❖

CHEWY COCONUT MACAROONS

A recipe for these chewy coconut macaroons appeared years ago on the package of Baker's Angel Flake Coconut.

1 ⅓ cups flake coconut, about
⅓ cup sugar
2 tablespoons flour
⅛ teaspoon salt
2 egg whites
½ teaspoon almond extract
Candied cherry halves, optional

Combine coconut, sugar, flour and salt in mixing bowl. Stir in egg whites and almond extract. Mix well. Drop by teaspoons onto lightly greased baking sheets. Garnish with candied cherry halves, if desired. Bake at 325 degrees 20 to 25 minutes until edges of cookies are golden brown. Remove from baking sheets immediately and cool on rack. Makes about 1½ dozen.

❖

CHINESE ALMOND COOKIES

This recipe was once shared by a Chinese chef whose name is now lost. But the pleasure of baking these authentic cookies lingers for hundreds of readers.

2 cups flour
½ teaspoon baking soda
¾ teaspoon baking powder
1 egg
½ pound lard
½ cup brown sugar, packed
½ cup granulated sugar
½ teaspoon almond extract
3 dozen blanched whole almonds, about
1 or 2 egg yolks

Sift flour with baking soda and baking powder. Beat egg and lard together. Add

Chinese Almond Cookies (continued)

sugars and almond extract. Gradually mix in dry ingredients until well blended.

For each cookie, roll 1 tablespoon dough into ball. Place on ungreased baking sheets and press almond in middle of each. Brush with beaten egg yolk and bake at 350 degrees 15 to 20 minutes. Makes about 3 dozen.

❖

SOFT MOLASSES GINGER COOKIES

These soft molasses cookies have always been in demand.

> *½ cup butter or margarine, softened*
> *½ cup sugar*
> *¾ cup molasses*
> *1 egg*
> *2 ½ cups flour*
> *1 ½ teaspoons ground ginger*
> *1 teaspoon ground cinnamon*
> *¼ teaspoon salt*
> *2 teaspoons baking soda*
> *¼ cup water*

Cream butter with sugar until light and fluffy. Beat in molasses and egg.

Sift flour with ginger, cinnamon and salt. Dissolve baking soda in water. Add flour and soda mixtures alternately to butter mixture, blending well after each addition.

Drop by tablespoon onto greased and floured baking sheet. Bake at 400 degrees 10 minutes or until done. Remove from baking sheet and cool on wire racks. Makes about 3 dozen.

❖

SHORTBREAD COOKIES

This traditional short and simple recipe becomes the basis for crescents, Mexican wedding cakes and Christmas cookies. They can be topped with icing and decorations.

½ pound butter, softened
½ cup powdered sugar
2 cups flour
¼ teaspoon salt

Cream butter in mixer until smooth. Add powdered sugar and beat until light and fluffy. Mix flour and salt and add to creamed mixture, mixing thoroughly.

Roll out dough until ¼-inch thick. Cut into rectangles about 1 x 2-inches. Place on ungreased baking sheet and pierce with tines of fork for decorative effect, if desired. Bake at 350 degrees 20 to 25 minutes or until lightly browned around edges. Cool on rack. Makes about 2 dozen.

CRESCENTS
Shape dough into crescent shapes of desired size. Place on cookie sheets and bake as instructed. Dust with powdered sugar while still warm.

MEXICAN WEDDING CAKES
Roll dough into balls, then roll in finely chopped walnuts or other nuts. Bake as directed.

CHRISTMAS COOKIES
Roll out dough to ¼-inch thickness. Cut in desired shapes using cookie cutters, a small glass or hand-drawn shapes. Bake as directed. Brush with icing and decorate with sprinkles or candied fruits.

❖

HERMITS

These brown sugar drop cookies are a basic part of a cookie lover's repertoire.

1 cup sifted flour
2 teaspoons baking powder
½ teaspoon salt
½ cup butter or margarine, softened
¾ cup brown sugar, packed
2 eggs
½ teaspoon vanilla
½ cup chopped nuts
1 cup golden raisins
2 cups bran flakes

Sift flour with baking powder and salt. Blend butter and brown sugar. Add eggs and vanilla. Add flour mixture with nuts, raisins and bran, mixing well. Drop by teaspoons onto ungreased baking sheets and bake at 375 degrees 11 minutes. Makes about 4 dozen.

❖

SNICKERDOODLES

These plain cookie balls rolled in cinnamon-sugar have appealed to generations of readers.

½ cup butter or margarine, softened
½ cup shortening
1 ½ cups plus 2 tablespoons sugar
2 eggs
1 ¾ cups flour
½ teaspoon cream of tartar
1 teaspoon baking soda
¼ teaspoon salt
2 teaspoons ground cinnamon

Thoroughly mix butter with shortening, 1½ cups sugar and eggs. Blend in flour, cream of tartar, baking soda and salt. Shape dough by rounded teaspoons into balls. Mix 2 remaining tablespoons sugar with cinnamon. Roll balls in mixture. Place 2 inches apart on ungreased baking sheet and bake at 400 degrees 8 to 10 minutes or until set. Remove from baking sheet immediately and cool on wire rack. Makes about 6 dozen cookies.

❖

PECAN-CARAMEL-CAKE MIX BROWNIES

Cookie recipes appearing on labels of baking products as these brownies did, often end up on the most-wanted request list.

1 pound caramels

2/3 cup evaporated milk

3/4 cup butter or margarine, softened

1 (18 1/2-ounce) package devil's-food cake mix

1 cup chopped pecans

1 (6-ounce) package semisweet chocolate pieces

1 cup pecan halves or chopped nuts

Combine caramels and 1/3 cup evaporated milk in top of double boiler. Melt over simmering water, stirring frequently. Keep in melted form.

Cream butter in large bowl until light and smooth. Beat in cake mix and remaining 1/3 cup evaporated milk. Stir in chopped pecans and chocolate pieces. Turn into greased 13 x 9-inch baking pan. Bake at 350 degrees 35 to 45 minutes or until cake tests done. Cool slightly.

Top with pecan halves and drizzle with caramel mixture. Or spread with caramel mixture and top with halved or chopped nuts. Makes about 15 brownies.

❖

LEMON-GLAZE BARS

Make these cookies without the pecans and coconut for a simple lemon bar cookie.

1 cup cake flour
2 tablespoons granulated sugar
⅛ teaspoon salt
⅓ cup butter or margarine, softened
2 eggs, lightly beaten
1 cup light brown sugar, packed
½ cup chopped pecans
1 cup flake coconut
1 tablespoon lemon juice
1 teaspoon grated lemon peel
Tart Lemon Glaze

Combine flour, granulated sugar and salt in mixing bowl. Cut in butter until mixture resembles coarse meal. Press mixture in bottom of 8- or 9-inch square pan. Bake at 350 degrees 15 minutes or until lightly browned.

Mix eggs, brown sugar, pecans, coconut, lemon juice and peel. Spread over baked pastry and bake at 350 degrees 25 to 30 minutes. Loosen around edges while warm. Top with Tart Lemon Glaze. Cool in pan. Cut into squares or bars. Makes 16 to 20 bars.

TART LEMON GLAZE

1 tablespoon lemon juice
⅔ cup sifted powdered sugar
1 teaspoon grated lemon peel

Gradually add lemon juice to sugar. Blend well and stir in lemon peel.

❖

GRANOLA BARS

An attempt to duplicate the popular cookie-confection resulted in this recipe.

6 tablespoons butter or margarine, softened
½ cup brown sugar, packed
¼ cup honey
1 egg
1 teaspoon vanilla
1 cup flour
½ teaspoon baking powder
½ teaspoon salt
¼ teaspoon baking soda
1 ½ cups bite-size crispy bran squares, crushed to measure ½ cup
½ cup raisins
½ cup flake coconut
¼ cup plus 3 tablespoons shelled sunflower seeds
2 tablespoons sesame seeds

Cream butter with brown sugar. Beat in honey, egg and vanilla.

Combine flour, baking powder, salt, baking soda and cereal. Add to creamed mixture. Stir in raisins, coconut and ¼ cup sunflower seeds.

Spread evenly in greased 13 x 9-inch baking pan. Sprinkle sesame seeds and remaining 3 tablespoons sunflower seeds evenly over top.

Bake at 350 degrees 15 to 20 minutes or until wood pick inserted in center comes out clean and top is lightly browned. Cool. Cut into bars. Makes 24 bars.

❖

ORIGINAL NANAIMO BARS

This recipe is usually requested by readers traveling to Nanaimo in Vancouver where these cookie bars are a specialty. To avoid using raw eggs in this no-bake bar cookie, we found a recipe in which the egg is part of a cooked custard.

¾ cup plus 1 tablespoon butter or margarine

¼ cup granulated sugar

1 egg

¼ cup unsweetened cocoa powder

2 cups graham cracker crumbs

1 cup shredded coconut

½ cup chopped nuts

3 tablespoons milk

2 tablespoons egg custard mix powder

2 cups sifted powdered sugar

4 (1-ounce) squares semisweet chocolate

Mix ½ cup butter, granulated sugar, egg and cocoa. Place in top of double boiler over simmering water and cook and stir until mixture resembles custard.

Combine crumbs, coconut and nuts. Add to cocoa mixture and blend well. Spread and press firmly into 9-inch-square pan. Cream ¼ cup butter, milk, custard powder and powdered sugar. Spread over mixture in pan.

Melt chocolate in top of double boiler over hot water. Add remaining 1 tablespoon butter and blend well. Spread over icing. Let stand until set. Refrigerate. Makes 27 (3 x 1-inch) bars.

❖

PEANUT BUTTER BARS

Public school food service archives are full of nostalgic recipes that readers crave and often request. A reader who attended Palos Verdes High School raved about these crumbly, chocolate-covered bar cookies—and so did our taste panel.

> 1 (16-ounce) jar peanut butter
> 2 eggs
> 1 ½ cups sugar
> ¼ cup butter or margarine, melted
> Chocolate Frosting

Combine peanut butter, eggs, sugar and butter in mixer bowl and mix at high speed to quickly blend well. Press peanut butter mixture into greased 9-inch square baking pan and bake at 325 degrees 15 to 20 minutes. Cover with Chocolate Frosting. Cut into bars. Makes 16 (2 x 3-inch) bars.

> **CHOCOLATE FROSTING**
>
> 2 ¼ cups powdered sugar
> 2 tablespoons unsweetened cocoa powder
> ½ teaspoon vanilla
> Water
> 2 tablespoons butter or margarine, softened

Combine sugar and cocoa in bowl. Mix thoroughly. Pour vanilla in measuring cup and add water to make ⅓ cup. Pour into sugar mixture and stir until smooth. Add butter and beat smooth with spoon or mixer, about 1 minute. Add few drops water if too stiff.

❖

MINCEMEAT-FILLED COOKIES

A favorite request for Christmas baking.

1 ½ cups shortening
¾ cup brown sugar, packed
¾ cup granulated sugar
1 egg
4 ½ tablespoons milk
1 ½ teaspoons vanilla
4 ½ cups sifted flour
¾ teaspoon salt
¾ teaspoon baking soda
1 (1-pound, 4-ounce) can mincemeat pie filling
½ cup orange marmalade

Cream shortening with sugars until fluffy. Add egg, milk and vanilla. Beat well. Sift flour with salt and baking soda and add to creamed mixture, mixing well. Wrap dough in wax paper and chill thoroughly.

Roll a quarter of dough at a time on floured surface to thickness of ⅛ inch. Cut with 2½-inch round cutter. Cut small hole in center of half of cookies with small cutter. Place whole circles 1-inch apart on ungreased baking sheet. Combine pie filling and marmalade and place 1 tablespoon of mixture on each cookie. Place circles with cutouts over filling and seal edges of cookie by pressing with fork. Bake at 375 degrees 10 to 12 minutes. Makes 4½ dozen.

❖

BISCOTTI

The rise in trattorias and coffeehouses caused an increase in requests for this Italian toasted biscuit and dunking cookie.

⅓ cup butter or margarine, softened
¾ cup sugar
3 eggs
¾ teaspoon ground anise seed
½ teaspoon salt
½ teaspoon almond extract
½ teaspoon vanilla
3 cups sifted flour
2 teaspoons baking powder
1 ¼ cups slivered blanched almonds

Cream butter with sugar. Add eggs, anise seed, salt, almond extract and vanilla and beat until light and fluffy.

Sift flour with baking powder and add to creamed mixture. Add almonds. Stir then knead until well blended.

Turn dough onto floured board. Divide into four equal portions. Shape each piece into slightly rounded loaf about 12 x 1½-inches. Place 3-inches apart on greased baking sheets. Bake at 325 degrees 20 to 30 minutes.

Remove from oven and immediately cut each loaf into 24 diagonal slices. Place slices cut side up on baking sheets. Toast under broiler turning to brown each side slightly. Makes 8 dozen.

PIES & PASTRIES

This chapter is a journey into the pies and pastries that have passed the test of time with our readers. They will give you a clue as to the tastes of readers from the fifties onward, because most of the recipes are old favorites to which readers rely on to please dinner party guests, in-laws, bosses, friends, relatives and children.

❖

Dear S.O.S.:
     Some time ago you printed a recipe for peanut butter pie. I've misplaced my recipe and would appreciate a repeat.
–Vivian

Dear Vivian:
     Dear S.O.S. readers love the peanut butter pie from La Quinta Hotel in La Quinta, California.

CITY RESTAURANT APPLE-CRANBERRY PIE

The former City Restaurant in Los Angeles does a wonderful job with dessert. This festive holiday pie was created by the Midwestern mother of chef Mary Sue Milliken, one of the owners of City Restaurant.

> *5 extra large Granny Smith apples*
> *1 (12-ounce) package cranberries*
> *1 ½ cups sugar*
> *¼ cup minute tapioca*
> *Partially Baked Pie Shell*
> *Streusel*

Peel, core and chop apples in pieces the size of cranberries. Place cranberries in food processor. Chop briefly, about 10 seconds.

Combine apples and cranberries in large bowl. Add sugar and stir until fruit is coated with sugar. Cover bowl and set aside until juices from fruit flow freely and sugar is almost completely dissolved, about 15 to 20 minutes.

Stir tapioca into fruit and juice and let stand 10 to 15 minutes or longer. Fill Partially Baked Pie Shell with apple-cranberry filling. Sprinkle top generously with Streusel. Reserve any remaining Streusel for other use. Bake at 325 degrees until filling bubbles in center, about 45 minutes. (If edges of pie shell begin to brown too quickly, cover with strips of foil.) Makes 1 (10-inch) pie.

PARTIALLY BAKED PIE SHELL

> *2 cups flour, softened*
> *½ cup lard, softened*
> *¼ cup unsalted butter*
> *1 teaspoon salt*
> *Ice water*

Combine flour, lard, butter and salt in large bowl. Lightly work dough using fingertips until pieces of butter and lard are no larger than small peas. Add ⅓ cup ice water, a little at a time, tossing flour mixture lightly with fork. If mixture seems too dry to press into ball, add another 1 tablespoon ice water.

Press mixture into ball. Wrap in plastic wrap and allow to rest about 30 minutes in refrigerator. Roll to ⅛-inch thickness. Fit into 10-inch pie plate. Flute edge attractively and let rest again in refrigerator 30 minutes. Line shell with sheet of foil

filled *City Restaurant Apple-Cranberry Pie (continued)*

filled with pastry weights or uncooked dry beans. Bake at 425 degrees until edges are light brown. Remove foil and weights. Return to oven until bottom crust is set and no longer appears raw.

STREUSEL

⅔ cup unsalted butter, softened
¾ cup light brown sugar, packed
½ teaspoon salt
1 teaspoon ground cinnamon
1 ½ cups flour

Combine butter, brown sugar, salt, cinnamon and flour. Lightly work mixture using fingertips until butter is completely incorporated and mixture is crumbly.

❖

HEAVENLY LEMON PIE

Bullock's Wilshire in Los Angeles no longer exists, but the extraordinary pie served at the department store tea room lives on.

4 eggs separated
½ cup sugar
Grated peel and juice of 1 large lemon
2 cups whipping cream, whipped
Meringue Crust
1 tablespoon powdered sugar

Beat egg yolks with sugar, lemon peel and juice until light. Cook, stirring, in top of double boiler over simmering water until thickened. Remove from heat and cool thoroughly.

Fold in half of whipped cream. Turn into Meringue Crust and refrigerate at least 2 hours to set. Fold powdered sugar into remaining whipped cream and spread over chilled pie. Makes 1 (9-inch) pie.

MERINGUE CRUST

4 egg whites
1 cup sugar
1 teaspoon lemon juice

Beat egg whites until soft peaks form. Gradually add sugar, beating until stiff but not dry. Blend in juice. Grease 9-inch pie pan generously. Spoon meringue mixture into pan and with spoon push mixture up around edges to form pie shell. Bake at 200 degrees 2 hours. Cool.

❖

KEY LIME PIE

When reader's request key lime pie, we give them this simple–and authentic–recipe.

2 (14-ounce) cans sweetened condensed milk
2 eggs
1 cup lime juice
1 (9-inch) baked single-crust pastry shell

Combine condensed milk and eggs in large bowl and blend well. Add lime juice. Pour into baked pie shell. Refrigerate several hours or overnight. Makes 1 (9-inch) pie.

PERSIMMON PIE

Use ripe persimmons to make mashing easy and a strainer to remove the fibers.

2 cups persimmon pulp
1 egg, beaten
1 cup milk
½ cup sugar
Dash salt
1 tablespoon cornstarch
1 (9-inch) unbaked single-crust pie shell

Mix persimmon pulp, egg and milk in bowl. In separate bowl. In separate bowl, mix sugar, salt and cornstarch. Combine sugar mixture and persimmon mixture. Pour filling into pie shell and bake at 450 degrees 10 minutes. Reduce heat to 350 degrees and bake 50 to 60 minutes longer. Makes 1 (9-inch) pie.

❖

FRENCH SILK CHOCOLATE PIE

Many readers fell in love with this silky smooth knock-off of a pie served at Baker's Square restaurant chain in California.

½ cup butter, cut into 8 parts
¾ cup sugar
1 (1-ounce) square unsweetened chocolate, melted and cooled
1 teaspoon vanilla
2 eggs
1 (8-inch) baked single-crust pie shell
Whipped cream

Cream butter and sugar until light in mixer bowl. Beat in chocolate and vanilla until blended. Add eggs, one at a time, and beat at medium speed 5 minutes after each addition. Turn into pastry shell. Chill. Garnish with whipped cream. Makes 1 (8-inch) pie.

❖

THE WILLOWS' COCONUT CREAM PIE

Reader's returning from Hawaii often request recipes from desserts tasted there. When they ask for coconut cream pie, we give them this one.

2 cups milk
½ cup sugar
Dash salt
Grated fresh coconut
4 egg yolks
3 tablespoons cornstarch
3 tablespoons water
1 tablespoon butter or margarine
1 teaspoon vanilla
1 (9-inch) baked single-crust pie shell
Meringue

Combine milk, sugar, salt and ¼ cup grated coconut in medium saucepan. Cook until mixture is very hot.

Beat egg yolks, then blend in cornstarch and water. Add egg yolk mixture to milk mixture. Cook and stir about 1 minute. Add butter and vanilla. Cool filling and pour into pie shell. Swirl meringue onto pie, making sure it is sealed to edge of pie shell. Sprinkle with grated coconut. Bake at 400 degrees until golden brown. Cool completely. Makes 1 (9-inch) pie.

MERINGUE

4 to 6 egg whites
¼ teaspoon cream of tartar
Sugar

Beat egg whites with cream of tartar until soft peaks form. Gradually add 1 tablespoon sugar for each egg white used and continue beating until soft peaks form.

❖

MILLIONAIRE PIE

Millionaire pie is an old—and we mean old—standby of past generations. We often publish this version from Clifton's Silver Spoon cafeteria chain in Los Angeles.

1 1/3 cups powdered sugar
1/3 cup butter or margarine, softened
1 egg
1/8 teaspoon salt
1/8 teaspoon vanilla
1 (8-inch) baked single-crust pastry shell
Topping
Sweetened whipped cream

Combine powdered sugar, butter, egg, salt and vanilla in bowl. Mix on low speed 15 minutes exactly. Spoon mixture evenly into pie shell. Spread Topping evenly over filled pie.

Using pastry tube, pipe ruffle of whipped cream around edge of pie to garnish. Chill at least 4 hours before serving. Makes 8 servings.

TOPPING

2/3 whipping cream
1/3 crushed pineapple, well-drained
1/3 cup chopped pecans

Whip cream until stiff. Fold in pineapple and nuts.

❖

GRASSHOPPER PIE

Reader's love serving this colorful pie for St. Patrick's Day.

⅔ cup milk
24 marshmallows
2 ounces green crème de menthe
1 ounce white crème de cacao
1 cup whipping cream
Chocolate Crust
Additional whipped cream, optional

Scald milk in top of double boiler over simmering water. Add marshmallows. Stir over simmering water until marshmallows are melted. Cool to room temperature. Add crème de menthe and crème de cacao.

Whip cream and fold into marshmallow mixture. Turn into Chocolate Crust and freeze. Serve with additional whipped cream, if wished. Makes 1 (9-inch) pie.

CHOCOLATE CRUST

1 ¼ cups crushed chocolate cookie wafers
⅓ melted butter

Mix chocolate wafers with melted butter. Pat evenly onto bottom and up sides of 9-inch pie pan. Chill.

❖

TRUCK STOP REECE PIE

The P&H Truck Stop restaurant in Wells River, Vermont, is famous for their "Reece" Pie made with flavors inspired by the popular peanut butter and chocolate candy.

¾ cup plus 3 tablespoons powdered sugar

½ cup peanut butter

1 (9-inch) baked single-crust or Graham cracker pie shell

1 (5 ⅛-ounce) package chocolate pudding mix

3 cups milk

2 tablespoons unsweetened cocoa powder

½ cup whipping cream, whipped

Chocolate sprinkles, optional

Combine ¾ cup powdered sugar and peanut butter, mixing well. Spread over bottom of pie shell, reserving 2 tablespoons for topping. If mixture is too stiff to spread, add small amount of warm water.

Prepare chocolate pudding according to package directions, using milk. Pour into pie crust over peanut butter layer and chill in refrigerator.

Sift cocoa into whipped cream and swirl. Spread over cooled pie. Blend remaining 3 tablespoons powdered sugar with reserved peanut butter topping and sprinkle over pie. Garnish with chocolate sprinkles. Makes 1 (9-inch) pie.

❖

LA QUINTA HOTEL PEANUT BUTTER PIE

This pie made with vanilla pudding mix flavored with peanut butter has been published annually since we received the recipe from the La Quinta Golf and Tennis Resort near Palm Springs in the seventies.

1 (4.6 ounces) package vanilla pudding mix

6 or 7 teaspoons peanut butter

½ cup whipping cream, whipped

1 (9-inch) baked single-crust pie shell or Graham cracker pie shell

Sweetened whipped cream, optional

¼ cup chopped peanuts, optional

Prepare pudding mix according to package directions, adding peanut butter. Beat until thoroughly blended. Cool.

Fold in whipping cream. Turn into baked pie shell. Chill until set. Top with sweetened whipped cream and sprinkle with peanuts. Makes 1 (9-inch) pie.

❖

SPAGO'S MACADAMIA NUT TART

The famous Spago in Los Angeles is the source of many recipes our readers have requested. Here's one for an outstanding macadamia nut tart.

⅓ cup brown sugar, packed
¼ cup granulated sugar
½ cup corn syrup
2 whole eggs
2 egg yolks
1 tablespoon butter
½ vanilla bean, split
1 ¼ tablespoons Frangelico liqueur
1 ½ cups toasted macadamia nuts, coarsely chopped
Tart Shell

Beat brown sugar, granulated sugar, corn syrup, eggs and egg yolks until light. Brown butter in saucepan with vanilla bean and Frangelico.

Discard vanilla bean and add butter mixture to sugar mixture. Fold in macadamia nuts. Pour into Tart Shell. Bake at 350 degrees for 30 minutes or until set. Makes 1 (10- or 12-inch) tart.

TART SHELL

3 cups pastry flour
½ cup sugar
2 cups butter
3 egg yolks
¼ cup whipping cream

Blend pastry flour, sugar and butter in heavy duty mixer fitted with dough hook

Spago's Macadamia Nut Tart (continued)

until crumbly. Beat egg yolks with whipping cream and add to flour mixture until dough is well mixed. Do not overmix.

Divide dough into 3 portions and chill. Reserving 2 portions for other use, roll out one portion and pat into 10- to 12-inch tart pan. Butter one side of wax paper square large enough to fit over pie shell and place, buttered side down, on uncooked pastry shell. Top wax paper with uncooked rice, dry beans or pie weights. Bake at 350 degrees 20 minutes or until sides begin to brown. Remove weights and wax paper and bake tart shell additional 5 to 10 minutes until bottom begins to brown.

Note: Amount of dough for three pies was given to reduce chance of destroying chemical balance of original pie dough recipe. Freeze other portions for use when needed.

❖

TRADER JOE'S HEROIC BAKLAVA

When this nut and honey pastry, baklava, became popular at Trader Joe's discount food and wine outlet, readers lost no time requesting the recipe.

> *1 pound phyllo dough*
> *½ pound margarine (preferably all-natural margarine), melted*
> *Nut Filling*
> *Syrup*

Unwrap phyllo dough and fold entire amount in half, like pages of book. Keep covered with dry kitchen towel while working. Turn over one sheet as if opening "book". Brush with melted margarine, using soft 1½- to 2-inch brush.

Continue turning sheets (pages) and brushing with margarine until ⅓ have been brushed with butter. Lay flat in bottom of buttered 13 x 9-inch baking pan. Cover with ½ of Nut Filling.

Brush another ⅓ of pages and place over nuts in pan, laying flat. Top with remaining Nut Filling. Brush remaining pages and lay flat on top. Brush top sheet with remaining margarine.

With sharp knife, score pastry into diamonds, without quite cutting through to bottom. (To make diagonals, cut parallel horizontal cuts across pan, then cross diagonally from one end of each horizontal line).

Bake at 350 degrees 35 to 40 minutes or until puffed, crisp and deep golden in color. Immediately remove from oven and pour cooled Syrup over baklava. Let Stand 4 hours. When cool, cut through to bottom layer in scored cuts. Makes about 24 pieces.

NUT FILLING

1 ½ pounds toasted, unsalted walnuts, coarsely chopped or ground
1 cup sugar
1 ½ teaspoons ground cinnamon
½ teaspoon ground cloves

Combine nuts, sugar, cinnamon and cloves.

SYRUP

1 cup honey
¾ cup water
¼ cup sugar
2 tablespoons lemon juice
1 small piece lemon peel
1 small piece orange peel
1-inch piece cinnamon stick

Combine honey, water, sugar, lemon juice, lemon and orange peels and cinnamon stick in saucepan. Simmer 10 minutes. When syrup has cooled, discard peels and cinnamon stick.

❖

ALLIGATORS

When alligators, a flattened pastry sweet bread filled with almond paste and pecans, came on the Los Angeles scene, coffee break hosts went wild over them. Viktor Benes Bakery, which supplies Gelson's markets in Los Angeles, is credited with one of the best alligators in town.

½ package dry yeast

1 cup warm milk (105 to 110 degrees)

3 tablespoons sugar

½ teaspoon salt

Butter

2 ½ cups flour, about

Alligator Filling

1 egg, beaten

60 to 80 pecan halves

Maple Icing

Mix yeast with about ½ cup warm milk. Add sugar, salt, 3 tablespoons melted butter, remaining ½ cup warm milk and flour. Mix well. Knead 6 to 8 minutes to make smooth dough. Let dough rest 30 minutes. Roll out on floured board into large rectangle.

Spread top with ¼ cup softened butter. Fold dough into thirds. Repeat 3 more times, using ¼ cup butter each time and allowing dough to rest 30 minutes before filling.

Divide dough into 2 equal portions. Using one portion at a time, roll dough as thinly as possible into 12 x 18-inch rectangle. Spread half of Alligator Filling on entire surface of dough, then fold lengthwise in thirds. Place on lightly greased baking sheet and brush with beaten egg. Decorate top with about 30 to 40 pecans halves. Let rest 15 minutes. Repeat with remaining dough and filling.

Bake at 375 degrees 20 to 30 minutes or until golden brown. While still hot, drizzle top with Maple Icing. Makes 2 alligators.

ALLIGATOR FILLING

1 cup sugar
1 (7-ounce) package ($\frac{3}{4}$ cup) almond paste
$\frac{3}{4}$ cup butter, softened
$\frac{1}{4}$ cup honey
1 tablespoon flour
1 $\frac{1}{2}$ cups ground pecans

Blend sugar with almond paste, butter and honey to form smooth paste. Stir in flour, then pecans. Makes about 2 cups.

MAPLE ICING

$\frac{1}{2}$ cup maple syrup
$\frac{1}{4}$ cup butter
2 cups sifted powdered sugar

Heat maple syrup and butter in small saucepan until butter melts. Add sugar, blending until smooth. Makes about 1 cup.

❖

PUDDINGS

Puddings are an old-fashioned dessert which often remind readers of desserts made by their mothers and grandmothers. Some have asked for recipes that date back to the early twentieth century. Surprisingly, we have located most of them. We also get requests from readers who travel and return home yearning for another bite of the bread pudding they had in Texas or a crème brûlée in Spokane. Restaurant chefs in other states love the visibility and are happy to share with us.

❖

Dear S.O.S.:
    I would appreciate a good recipe for persimmon pudding.
—Anna

Dear Anna:
    Readers most often request the persimmon pudding shared by Mrs. Ronald Reagan.

BRENNAN'S BREAD PUDDING WITH WHISKY SAUCE

Probably the most popular and frequently requested bread pudding recipe is this one from Brennan's branch in Houston, Texas.

10 slices day-old French bread, torn
4 cups scalded milk
1 cup whipping cream
5 eggs
1 cup brown sugar, packed
2 teaspoons vanilla
1 teaspoon ground cinnamon
½ teaspoon ground nutmeg
¼ cup butter or margarine, melted
½ cup raisins
½ cup whole pecans
Whisky Sauce

Combine bread, milk and cream. Beat eggs, add sugar and mix well. Stir in bread mixture and add vanilla, cinnamon and nutmeg. Stir in butter, raisins and pecans. Turn into buttered 2-quart baking dish. Set in pan filled with warm water to about 1-inch deep. Bake at 350 degrees 1 hour or until knife inserted in center comes out clean. Serve with Whisky Sauce. Makes 8 servings.

WHISKY SAUCE

3 egg yolks
1 cup sugar
1 teaspoon vanilla
1 ½ cups milk
1 tablespoon cornstarch
¼ cup water
1 ½ ounces brandy

In saucepan lightly beat egg yolks, then add sugar, vanilla and milk and blend well. Cook over low heat until mixture comes to boil. Blend cornstarch in water and stir into hot mixture. Continue to cook until thickened. Remove from heat and stir in brandy. Cool.

GRAPE-NUTS PUDDING

If there is an old-time pudding more popular than this classic recipe originally printed on a box of Grape-Nuts cereal, we'd like to see it.

4 eggs
¼ cup sugar
¼ teaspoon salt
Milk
1 teaspoon vanilla
Grape-Nuts cereal
1 (3 ¾-ounce) package instant vanilla pudding mix

Lightly beat eggs and combine with sugar and salt. Beat until thick.

Scald 2 cups milk and add to eggs gradually, stirring constantly. Stir in vanilla. Sprinkle cereal into 5 to 6 greased custard cups or greased 1-quart baking dish to form ⅛-inch layer. Pour custard mixture into prepared cups and bake at 325 degrees 40 to 45 minutes for cup custard or 1 hour for large custard. Cool slightly.

Prepare instant pudding according to package directions, then dilute to thick sauce consistency with additional milk, as needed. Turn custards out onto serving dishes and serve topped with vanilla sauce. Makes 5 to 6 servings.

❖

MRS. REAGAN'S PERSIMMON PUDDING

Readers who have requested this recipe over the years (even after the Reagan's left the White House) consider it the best persimmon pudding around.

1 cup sugar
½ cup butter, melted
¼ teaspoon salt
1 cup flour, sifted
¼ teaspoon ground cinnamon
¼ teaspoon ground nutmeg
1 cup puréed persimmon pulp (3 to 4 very ripe fruit)
2 teaspoons baking soda
2 teaspoons warm water
Brandy
1 teaspoon vanilla
2 eggs, lightly beaten
1 cup raisins
½ cup chopped walnuts, optional
Brandy Whipped Cream Sauce

Stir sugar into melted butter. Resift flour with salt, cinnamon and nutmeg. Add to butter mixture. Stir in persimmon pulp. Dissolve baking soda in warm water. Add to mixture with 3 tablespoons brandy and vanilla. Add eggs, mixing lightly but thoroughly. Add raisins and nuts, stirring just until mixed.

Turn into buttered 5- to 6-cup heat-proof mold. Cover and place on rack in kettle. Pour in enough boiling water to reach halfway up sides of mold. Cover kettle and simmer 2½ to 3 hours. Let stand few minutes.

Unmold onto serving dish. Pour about ¼ cup warmed brandy over pudding and carefully ignite flame. Serve with Brandy Whipped Cream Sauce. Makes 6 to 8 servings. *(continued)*

Mrs. Reagan's Persimmon Pudding (continued)

BRANDY WHIPPED CREAM SAUCE

1 egg
½ cup butter, melted
1 cup sifted powdered sugar
Dash salt
1 tablespoon brandy flavoring
1 cup whipping cream

Beat egg until light and fluffy. Beat in butter, powdered sugar, salt and brandy flavoring. Whip cream until stiff. Gently fold into egg mixture. Cover and chill.

❖

DURGIN-PARK BAKED INDIAN PUDDING

Readers visiting Boston often return with a request for this unusual molasses pudding.

1 cup yellow cornmeal
½ cup black molasses
¼ cup sugar
¼ cup lard or butter
¼ teaspoon salt
¼ teaspoon baking soda
2 eggs
1 ½ quarts hot milk

Mix cornmeal, molasses, sugar, lard or butter, salt, baking soda and eggs with half of milk (3 cups). Pour into greased soufflé dish or baking pan and bake until mixture comes to boil. Stir in remaining hot milk and bake at 375 degrees 3½ hours. Makes about 8 servings.

❖

WALDORF ASTORIA RICE PUDDING

The Waldorf Astoria Starlight Room chef shared this recipe with our readers in 1978, and it has been a favorite ever since.

1 cup plus 2 tablespoons short-grain rice
2 ½ quarts milk
1 ¼ cups sugar
¼ teaspoon salt
¾ cup raisins
Vanilla
1 cup whipping cream
2 egg yolks

Rinse rice in cold running water. Drain well.

Combine milk with ⅓ of sugar and salt and bring to boil. Add rice, reduce heat and simmer, covered, 1 hour or until rice is soft, stirring occasionally. Add raisins, remaining sugar and vanilla to taste.

Turn mixture into oven-proof serving dish or individual pudding cups. Beat cream until soft. Add egg yolks and stir well. Spread mixture evenly over top of rice pudding. Place under broiler until browned on top, being careful cream does not scorch. Makes 6 to 8 servings.

❖

CUSTARD LULU

This *Dear S.O.S.* favorite of favorites has been around for years in many forms. This one is made with a bottled caramel fudge topping.

4 eggs
1 cup sugar
2 cups milk
½ teaspoon ground nutmeg
1 ½ teaspoons vanilla
6 tablespoons bottled caramel fudge topping

Beat eggs with sugar 5 minutes. Add milk, nutmeg and vanilla. Place 1 tablespoon caramel fudge topping in bottom of each of 6 custard cups. Fill prepared cups with

Custard Lulu (continued)

custard mixture and place cups in pan of hot water. Bake at 400 degrees 30 minutes until firm or until knife inserted in center comes out clean. Makes 6 servings.

Note: If desired, omit caramel fudge topping and serve with whipped cream sprinkled with graham cracker crumbs.

❖

CHOCOLATE CRÈME BRÛLÉE

Joachim Splichal, chef-owner of Pinot and Patina in Los Angeles, shared this recipe with our readers.

> *1 quart whipping cream*
> *2 cups milk*
> *1 cup granulated sugar*
> *1 vanilla bean, split*
> *10 egg yolks*
> *9 ounces fine-quality dark sweet chocolate (such as Valbrona or other fine dark chocolate), melted*
> *Raw sugar*

Combine cream, milk, ½ cup sugar and vanilla bean in saucepan. Bring to boil over medium heat.

Mix yolks with remaining ½ cup sugar. Add ½ cup milk mixture to egg mixture to temper. Then pour egg mixture into remaining milk mixture and stir. Add melted chocolate and stir to mix. Strain.

Pour into 8 (1-cup) ramekins. Place ramekins in another pan filled halfway with water and bake at 275 degrees 45 minutes.

Refrigerate until set. Sprinkle with raw sugar. Place ramekins under broiler until sugar melts. Makes 8 servings.

❖

CLINKERDAGGER'S BURNT CREAM

Clinkerdagger's, located in Spokane, Washington, provided one of the easiest and best custards in our file.

1 pint whipping cream
4 egg yolks
½ cup sugar
1 tablespoon vanilla
Sugar Topping

Heat whipping cream over low heat until it bubbles around edge of pan.

Beat egg yolks and sugar until thick, about 3 minutes. Gradually beat cream into egg yolks. Stir in vanilla and pour into 6 (6-ounce) custard cups. Place custard cups in baking pan with about ½ inch water in bottom. Bake at 350 degrees 20 to 25 minutes.

Remove from water and refrigerate until chilled. Sprinkle each custard with about 2 teaspoons Sugar Topping. Place on top rack under broiler and cook until topping is bubbly and brown, but not scorched. Chill before serving. Makes 6 servings.

SUGAR TOPPING

¼ cup granulated sugar
1 teaspoon brown sugar

Combine sugars and mix well.

❖

LAWRY'S ENGLISH TRIFLE

This English trifle served at Lawry's Prime Rib in Hollywood is a centerpiece dessert that looks beautiful in a glass punch bowl.

1 (4.6-ounce) package vanilla pudding and pie filling mix

2 cups half and half

2 tablespoons dark rum

2 ¼ cups whipping cream

3 tablespoons sugar

2 tablespoons red raspberry preserves

1 (10-inch) round sponge cake layer

¼ cup brandy

¼ cup dry sherry

30 strawberries

Combine pudding mix and half and half. Cook, stirring, until mixture comes to boil and thickens. Add rum and chill.

Whip 1¼ cups whipping cream and 1 tablespoon sugar until stiff. Fold into chilled pudding.

Coat inside of deep 10-inch bowl with raspberry preserves to within 1 inch of top. Slice cake horizontally into fourths. Place top slice, crust side up, in bottom of bowl, curving edges of cake upward.

Combine brandy and sherry. Sprinkle about 2 tablespoons mixture over cake slice. Spread ⅓ chilled pudding mix over cake slice. Repeat procedure 2 more times.

Arrange 15 strawberries on top layer of pudding. Cover with remaining cake layer, crust side down. Sprinkle with remaining brandy-sherry mixture.

Whip remaining 1 cup cream and 2 tablespoons sugar until stiff. Place whipped cream in pastry bag fitted with star tip. Pipe 12 mounds around edge of bowl and 3 mounds across diameter. Top each mound with strawberry. Chill at least 6 hours. Makes 12 servings.

Frozen Desserts

Fried Mexican ice cream surprises everyone. A hot and crispy shell actually seals a scoop of cold ice cream. *Kansas City Ice Cream* has been a reader favorite because the recipe is flawless no matter which flavor version you choose. One of our favorites–peach–is here. Readers bless a mother who provided us with a frozen chocolate dessert her children (and then their children) love to make. And there is frozen pie that tastes and feels just like a popular peanut butter candy. You'll love them all.

❖

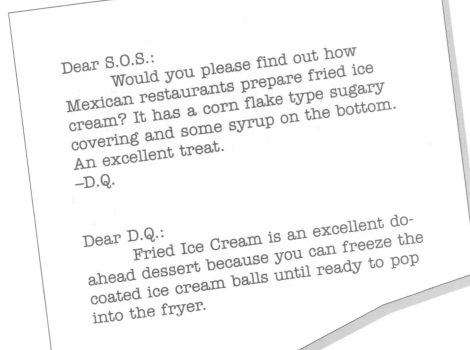

Dear S.O.S.:
Would you please find out how Mexican restaurants prepare fried ice cream? It has a corn flake type sugary covering and some syrup on the bottom. An excellent treat.
–D.Q.

Dear D.Q.:
Fried Ice Cream is an excellent do-ahead dessert because you can freeze the coated ice cream balls until ready to pop into the fryer.

EL TORITO'S DEEP-FRIED ICE CREAM

Deep-fried ice cream was popularized by Mexican restaurant chains in the Southwest during the last decade. It's a wonderful dessert to prepare in advance (except for last minute frying) for entertaining.

20 ounces chocolate chip ice cream

2 cups 4-grain flake cereal, crushed

1 ½ tablespoons sugar

3 ½ teaspoons ground cinnamon

2 eggs

1 teaspoon water

4 (8-inch) flour tortillas

Oil for deep-frying

Cinnamon-Sugar

Whipped cream

4 maraschino cherries

Form ice cream into 4 balls. Place in baking pan and freeze solid, 2 hours or longer. Mix cereal, sugar and cinnamon. Divide equally between 2 pie plates or other shallow containers. Beat eggs with water.

Roll each ice cream ball in cereal mixture and press coating into ice cream. Dip coated ball in egg wash, then roll in second container of cereal mixture. Again press coating onto ice cream. Freeze coated ice cream balls solid, 4 to 6 hours.

To make each tortilla container, cut off curved slice from 2 opposite sides to create a narrow waist. One end will serve as base for ice cream. Other end will be decorative fan.

Heat oil. Place tortilla between 2 ladles or large spoons of different sizes (smaller ladle on top). Place tortilla so that one end is cupped in larger ladle to form basket, with back of upper fan supported by handle of larger ladle. Deep fry until crisp. Drain and sprinkle with cinnamon-sugar. Place each fried tortilla in large-stemmed glass with fan part of tortilla standing vertically above glass.

Deep fry frozen coated ice cream balls 30 to 45 seconds. Set fried ice cream balls in base of tortillas. Top with dollops of whipped cream and decorate with cherries. Makes 4 servings.

❖

KANSAS CITY VANILLA ICE CREAM

This recipe was originally from a Kansas City reader who had gone to great pains to come up with texture and flavor that's always pleasing.

3 tablespoons cornstarch
6 cups milk
2 ⅔ cups sugar
4 large or 5 small eggs
¾ teaspoon salt
1 (13-ounce) can evaporated milk
1 pint whipping cream
3 ½ tablespoons vanilla
25 pounds crushed ice
Ice cream salt

Mix cornstarch with ½ cup milk until smooth. Add additional 1½ cups milk and cook in top of double boiler over simmering water until thick and smooth, stirring constantly to avoid lumps.

Blend sugar, eggs, salt and evaporated milk in electric mixer. Add hot cornstarch mixture and beat well. Add whipping cream, remaining 4 cups milk and vanilla.

Pour into 1-gallon electric or hand freezer. Pack with alternate layers of crushed ice and ice cream salt until entirely covered. Freeze according to manufacturer's directions until firm and remove paddle. Be sure to pour off excess water. Add mor crushed ice and salt as needed. Makes 1 gallon.

VARIATIONS:

BERRY ICE CREAM
Add 2 cups crushed fresh raspberries or blueberries and omit vanilla. It may be necessary to increase amount of sugar slightly.

CHOCOLATE ICE CREAM
Add 2 squares melted chocolate and omit vanilla.

FRESH PEACH ICE CREAM
Add 2 cups crushed ripe peaches. Use 1 tablespoon vanilla and ½ teaspoon almond extract.

Kansas City Vanilla Ice Cream (continued)

BANANA ICE CREAM
Add 2 cups mashed ripe bananas and 1 tablespoon vanilla. Omit evaporated milk.

COFFEE ICE CREAM
Dissolve 3 tablespoons instant coffee in 1 cup water. Use 2 tablespoons vanilla.

PUMPKIN ICE CREAM
Add 2 cups canned pumpkin. Use 1 tablespoon vanilla and add ½ teaspoon ground cinnamon.

❖

SOFT HOME-STYLE FROZEN YOGURT

Many shops now sell flavored frozen yogurt as a lower-fat alternative to ice cream. Here's how to make it at home using an ice cream maker.

> *1 pint whole-milk yogurt*
> *5 tablespoons fruit preserves*
> *¼ cup light corn syrup*

Combine yogurt, preserves and corn syrup. Mix thoroughly. Chill 2 to 3 hours. Freeze in ice cream maker according to manufacturer's directions. Makes 3 cups.

❖

FROZEN ALMOND TOFU DESSERT

High in protein and low in fat and cholesterol, tofu "ice cream" is the answer for health-conscious dessert lovers.

> *1 (30-ounce) carton soy bean pudding*
> *⅔ cup honey*
> *2 teaspoons almond extract*

Whip soy bean pudding until smooth and creamy. Add honey and almond extract. Process in ice cream maker according to manufacturer's directions. Makes about 1 quart.

CHART HOUSE MUD PIE

Steak houses, such as the Chart House chain on the West Coast, serve this ice cream pie topped with fudge, even though its origin is Southern.

⅔ (9-ounce) package dark chocolate wafers
¼ cup butter or margarine, softened
½ gallon coffee ice cream, softened slightly
¾ cup Chocolate Fudge Sauce
Whipped cream
Toasted sliced almonds

Crush wafers and mix with butter. Press into bottom and up sides of 9-inch pie plate. Chill thoroughly or bake at 350 degrees 7 minutes, then chill. Pack ice cream into chilled crust, shaping into slight mound. Freeze until firm. (Freezing before adding fudge sauce is essential to keep fudge from slipping off.) Pour fudge sauce evenly over pie and freeze until ready to serve. Serve with whipped cream and sprinkle with almond slices. Makes about 8 servings.

CHOCOLATE FUDGE SAUCE

5 squares unsweetened Swiss chocolate
½ cup butter or margarine
1 (5.3 ounce) can evaporated milk
3 cups powdered sugar
1 ¼ teaspoons vanilla

Melt chocolate and butter in small saucepan. Remove from heat and mix in milk alternately with powdered sugar. Bring to boil over medium heat, stirring constantly. Cook and stir 8 minutes or until thickened and creamy. Remove from heat and stir in vanilla. Store in refrigerator and use as needed. Makes 3 cups.

❖

VELVET TURTLE PIE

Readers dining at the Velvet Turtle chain restaurants in Southern California are often dazzled by their extraordinarily rich pie.

> *2 quarts almond praline ice cream*
> *Crumb Crust*
> *Caramel Fudge Sauce*
> *Hazelnut Meringue*

Soften praline ice cream in refrigerator. Pack 1 quart evenly into Crumb Crust. Drizzle with $\frac{1}{4}$ cup Caramel Fudge Sauce. Top with Hazelnut Meringue layer, trimming, if necessary, to leave $\frac{1}{2}$-inch border between pie and meringue.

Pack remaining quart ice cream into pie pan, filling in space between pan and meringue. Don't press hard or meringue will break. Cover with plastic wrap or wax paper and freeze at least 8 to 10 hours before serving. Swirl additional Caramel Fudge Sauce over top, if desired, or serve on side. Makes 1 (9-inch) pie.

CRUMB CRUST

> *6 ounces ground pecan cookies (about 11 cookies)*
> *$\frac{1}{2}$ cup ground hazelnuts*
> *1 teaspoon ground cinnamon*
> *$\frac{1}{4}$ cup melted butter*

Mix cookies, nuts and cinnamon. Mix butter into crumb mixture to incorporate evenly. Press into 9-inch springform pan, bringing crust $1\frac{1}{2}$-inches up sides. Chill until firm. Bake at 375 degrees 10 to 15 minutes. Cool, then freeze 2 hours.

HAZELNUT MERINGUE

> *4 egg whites*
> *Dash cream of tartar*
> *$\frac{3}{4}$ cup sugar*
> *$\frac{1}{4}$ cup plus 1 tablespoon ground hazelnuts*
> *$\frac{1}{4}$ teaspoon ground cinnamon*

Beat egg whites until foamy. Add cream of tartar and continue to beat until until whites are glossy. Gradually add sugar until well incorporated. Beat until whites are glossy and hold stiff peaks. Fold in ground nuts and cinnamon until well blended. Do not overmix. Pipe onto parchment paper to make 8-inch round and ½-inch thick. Bake at 250 degrees 1½- to 2 hours. Let stand in oven overnight. Peel off parchment and lift meringue off carefully. Makes 1 meringue layer.

CARAMEL FUDGE SAUCE

3 cups sugar
1 ¼ cups water
3 cups whipping cream
1 cup unsalted butter

Heat sugar in heavy saucepan over high heat. Stir with wooden spoon constantly until sugar caramelizes, about 8 to 10 minutes. Be careful not to overbrown. Carefully whisk in water.

Boil whipping cream until reduced to 1¾ cups. Add 1½ cups caramel mixture. Bring to boil. Stir in butter until melted. Boil until caramelized sugar dissolves completely, about 4 to 5 minutes. Use sauce as directed and reserve remaining sauce as dessert topping. Store in covered jar for use as desired. Makes about 4 cups sauce.

DESSERT SOUFFLÉS

These light and fluffy baked dishes made with egg yolks and beaten egg whites are heavenly dessert soufflés sometimes made with chocolate, liqueurs and fruits. French bistros prepare the basic batter ahead of time but don't start baking until a customer has ordered a soufflé. It's important for your oven temperature to be correct and to use the appropriate size soufflé dish.

❖

Dear S.O.S.:
     Recently I enjoyed the Cappucino Souffle at L'Escoffier in the Beverly Hilton. Would they pass along their recipe?
–Naomi

Dear Naomi:
     Most obligingly.

BISTRO CHOCOLATE SOUFFLÉ

Even though the original Bistro Restaurant in Beverly Hills is closed, the legacy of this extraordinary chocolate soufflé lives on in their Bistro Garden restaurant. It is the most popular dessert on the menu.

5 egg yolks

¾ cup granulated sugar

4 drops vanilla

1 cup flour

2 cups milk

2 ounces unsweetened chocolate, melted

8 egg whites

Additional granulated sugar

Powdered sugar

Sweetened whipped cream

Beat egg yolks with ½ cup sugar and vanilla until light and fluffy. Gradually beat in flour until paste is formed.

Meanwhile, bring milk to boil. Add egg mixture all at once to milk, bring again to boil and with heavy wire whisk quickly and vigorously beat until paste is well incorporated into milk and mixture is smooth. Continue to stir with wooden spoon until mixture is thick as light choux paste or pastry cream. Add melted chocolate and stir until blended. Cool.

Beat 3 egg whites with ⅓ of remaining sugar until light and frothy. Add 3 more egg whites and half of remaining sugar. Continue beating until sugar is incorporated. Add remaining 2 egg whites and remaining sugar and beat until whites are stiff and shiny but not dry. Egg whites should not slide if bowl is tipped. Fold egg whites into soufflé batter. Pipe or spoon into 12 greased and granulated sugar-coated 2-inch soufflé dishes or custard cups or 2 (5-inch) soufflé dishes and bake at 350 degrees 30 minutes for individual soufflés or 1 hour or longer for large soufflés. Dust with powdered sugar and serve topped with sweetened whipped cream. Makes 12 servings.

❖

HARRY'S CHOCOLATE CAPPUCCINO SOUFFLÉ

The popularity of cappuccino in the seventies started a lasting trend in cappuccino-flavored desserts, such as this soufflé from Harry's Bar in Century City, California.

1 ½ cups milk
2 tablespoons ground milk chocolate (preferably Ghirardelli)
1 tablespoon instant espresso coffee powder
1 tablespoon brown sugar, packed
¼ cup melted butter
2 tablespoons flour
6 egg whites
Granulated sugar
2 tablespoons powdered sugar
Espresso Sauce

In medium saucepan, combine milk, chocolate, espresso powder and brown sugar. Bring to boil over medium heat. In mixing bowl combine melted butter and flour. Mix until smooth. Slowly add to coffee mixture until well mixed. Set aside.

In large mixing bowl, beat egg whites (save eggs yolks for another use) until foamy, about 3 minutes. Add coffee mixture and mix until evenly colored. Pour mixture into 5 greased and sugared 5-ounce ceramic soufflé dishes. Level off to prevent overflowing. Place cups on baking sheet and bake at 375 degrees 15 minutes. Remove tray of soufflés from oven and sprinkle with powdered sugar.

To serve, cut into soufflés with knife and pour Espresso Sauce into soufflés until they puff to maximum height without spilling. Makes 5 soufflés.

ESPRESSO SAUCE

2 cups heavy whipping cream
2 tablespoons ground milk chocolate
1 tablespoon instant espresso coffee powder
3 tablespoons brown sugar, packed

Combine whipping cream, chocolate, espresso powder and brown sugar in saucepan. Heat until consistency of syrup.

❖

CONFECTIONS

Making your own sweets successfully requires patience and the skill that comes from experience. Many of our readers are gifted candy-makers who carefully follow recipe instructions and know that an accurate candy thermometer is essential. Making candy, particularly fudge, is also an enjoyable first cooking experience for children. We have several fudge recipes and other favorite requests including peanut butter crunch and chocolate truffles.

❖

Dear S.O.S.:
My sister made a treat called Vinegar Candy. It has a delicious sweet and sour taste and has the appearance of a peanut brittle. Perhaps your readers can help.
—Clifford

Dear Clifford:
We can help. The recipe is an annual favorite.

APRICOT JELLIES

Requests for this sweet preparation begin around Christmas. They can be decoratively packaged and given as gifts.

2 envelopes unflavored gelatin
1 1/2 cups sugar
1/8 teaspoon salt
8 ounces dried apricots (about 2 1/4 cups)
1/2 cup water
1/2 teaspoon vanilla
1/2 cup chopped walnuts
Powdered sugar

Combine gelatin, sugar and salt in top of double boiler. Purée apricots with water in blender. Add apricot purée to gelatin mixture and cook over simmering water 30 minutes, stirring often. Remove from heat and stir in vanilla and nuts.

Pour mixture into 8 x 4-inch loaf pan that has been rinsed with cold water. Let stand in cool place overnight. Loosen candy around edges with sharp knife. Turn out onto board dusted with powdered sugar and cut into small cubes, then roll in powdered sugar. Makes 40 cubes.

MOM'S BOURBON BALLS

A Christmas season wouldn't be complete without sampling a Bourbon Ball in someone's home or receiving a gift of these confections. They can be prepared as 1-inch balls or packed into a robust 4-inch ball wrapped in bourbon-soaked cheesecloth.

1 cup ground pecans or walnuts
Powdered sugar
1 ½ tablespoons unsweetened cocoa powder
3 ½ cups crushed vanilla wafers
½ cup bourbon
3 tablespoons light corn syrup

Combine nuts, 1 cup powdered sugar, cocoa and wafer crumbs and blend well. Stir in bourbon and corn syrup.

Form mixture into 1-inch balls. Roll in powdered sugar and store in tightly covered container. If desired, bourbon balls can be wrapped in double piece of cheesecloth that has been soaked in bourbon and wrung out. Makes 3 dozen.

❖

CITY SCHOOL PEANUT BUTTER CRUNCH

Angelenos who attended city schools never seem to forget these crunchy squares.

2 ½ cups sugar
1 ½ cups light corn syrup
3 cups peanut butter, warmed
1 ¼ (12-ounce) packages cornflakes

Combine sugar and syrup in saucepan. Bring to rapid boil, stirring constantly. Do not overcook. Remove from heat and add warm peanut butter. Stir until well mixed. Pour over cornflakes. Mix well, working quickly. (It's best to have some help with this stage of operation as quickness is essential to prevent candy from hardening.) Pour into well-greased 15½ x 10½-inch pan, pressing lightly. Cut into squares. Makes about 24 squares.

❖

JIMMY CARTER'S FAVORITE PEANUT BRITTLE

Jimmy Carter made this standard but good peanut brittle recipe famous when he took office. It's still famous with our readers.

> *3 cups sugar*
> *1 ½ cups water*
> *1 cup light corn syrup*
> *3 cups peanuts*
> *2 tablespoons baking soda*
> *¼ cup butter*
> *1 teaspoon vanilla*

Bring sugar, water and syrup to boil and boil until it spins thread or syrup reaches 230 to 234 degrees on candy thermometer. Add peanuts and cook and stir continuously until syrup turns golden brown. Remove from heat and add baking soda, butter and vanilla. Stir until butter melts. Pour onto 2 baking sheets with sides. As mixture begins to harden around edges, pull until thin. Break into pieces. Makes about 1 pound.

❖

VINEGAR CANDY

Don't sour on these candies also known as Sponge or Honeycomb. They've been a *Dear S.O.S.* reader favorite for several decades. Just keep an eye on the candy thermometer and the rest is easy.

> *2 tablespoons butter or margarine*
> *2 cups sugar*
> *½ cup vinegar*

Melt butter in heavy pan and add sugar and vinegar. Stir until sugar is dissolved. Wipe down side of pan with pastry brush or cloth dipped in cold water. Boil until mixture reaches brittle stage, 256 degrees on candy thermometer. Cool on platter until easy to handle. Pull until transparent and cut into small pieces with scissors or sharp knife. Cool on buttered plates. Makes 1¼ pounds.

CHOCOLATE TRUFFLES

The recipe for these chocolate truffles evolved from the many suggestions and recipes sent in by our readers. They are easy and they are celestial.

2 tablespoons butter or margarine, softened
1 egg yolk
¼ cup powdered sugar
1 (4-ounce) package dark, bittersweet cooking chocolate, grated
1 tablespoon rum, optional
½ cup flake coconut, optional
Grated chocolate, chocolate sprinkles or ground nuts

Cream butter, then blend in egg yolk. Gradually add powdered sugar, blending well. Add cooking chocolate, rum and coconut. Mix well. Shape into ½-inch balls and roll in chocolate, chocolate sprinkles or ground nuts. Place on wax paper and chill several hours. Makes 24 candies.

❖

MAMIE EISENHOWER'S FUDGE

Million Dollar Fudge, the original name for this fudge, became even more famous and more in demand when shared by former First Lady, Mamie Eisenhower.

4 ½ cups sugar
2 tablespoons butter or margarine
Dash salt
1 (13-ounce) can evaporated milk
1 (12-ounce) package semisweet chocolate pieces
3 (4-ounce) packages sweet cooking chocolate, broken
2 cups marshmallow cream
2 cups chopped walnuts or pecans.

Combine sugar, butter, salt and milk in large saucepan. Bring to boil over medium heat, stirring constantly. Boil 6 minutes, stirring occasionally. Combine chocolates, marshmallow cream and nuts in mixing bowl. Pour milk mixture over chocolate and beat until chocolate is melted.

Turn into well-greased 13 x 9-inch pan. Cool several hours or until firm. Cut into squares and store in airtight container. Makes about 5 pounds.

PEANUT BUTTER FUDGE

Many readers have difficulties making candy because of sensitive temperature considerations. Using a candy thermometer helps increase chances of success. In this recipe, soft ball stage, 234 to 240 degrees, on the candy thermometer, means that a drop of candy forms into a soft, shiny ball when tested by dropping small amount of hot mixture into cup of cold water.

> *2 cups sugar*
> *Dash salt*
> *¾ cup milk or half and half*
> *2 tablespoons light corn syrup*
> *¼ cup peanut butter*
> *1 teaspoon vanilla*

Combine sugar, salt, milk and corn syrup in saucepan. Cook to soft-ball stage, 234 degrees on candy thermometer. Cool to lukewarm and add peanut butter and vanilla. Beat until creamy and pour into lightly greased 8-inch square pan. Cut into squares when cool. Makes about 1 pound.

❖

MYSTERY FUDGE

We don't know where this recipe originated, but readers think it resembles the fudge they buy in a candy store and that it's the best we've printed.

> *½ cup butter*
> *1 (6-ounce) package semisweet chocolate pieces*
> *1 teaspoon vanilla*
> *2 cups sugar*
> *1 (5 ¾-ounce) can evaporated milk*
> *10 large marshmallows*
> *1 cup chopped nuts*

Combine butter, chocolate pieces and vanilla in medium bowl. Set aside.

Place sugar, evaporated milk and marshmallows in medium saucepan. Bring to boil over medium heat, stirring frequently. Reduce heat to low and cook 6 minutes, stirring constantly.

Pour hot mixture over ingredients in bowl. Beat with electric mixer until fudge is thick and dull (this doesn't take long). Stir in nuts.

Pour into 8-inch square baking pan. Refrigerate several hours to firm. Cut into squares. Makes about 36 squares.

❖

CHOCOLATE NUT CHEWIES

The combination of nuts, chocolate and caramel make these smooth, chewy candies a favorite with readers and their children, who often write us for the recipe.

¾ cup sugar

2 tablespoons water

1 cup light corn syrup

¼ cup butter or margarine

¾ cup evaporated milk

½ teaspoon salt

⅛ teaspoon vanilla

Pecans halves

1 (6-ounce) package semisweet chocolate pieces, melted

Combine sugar, water and corn syrup and cook over medium heat until mixture comes to boil. Wash sugar crystals down from sides of pan with fork wrapped in dampened cheesecloth or pastry brush dipped in water. Add butter. When mixture starts to boil again, add milk very slowly, stirring constantly. It should take 5 minutes to add milk. Continue to cook until mixture reaches 244 degrees on candy thermometer or medium ball stage. Remove from heat and add salt and vanilla.

Cool slightly. Place pecans halves on baking sheet to form head and legs of turtles. Spoon caramel over nuts to form body. The caramel drops should be no larger than a quarter or turtles will be too large. When caramel has cooled, place Turtles on racks and cool completely. Spread chocolate over caramel and let set. Makes 8 dozen.

❖

ROCKY ROAD S'MORE'S

There isn't a Girl or Boy Scout or *Dear S.O.S.* reader who doesn't know about S'Mores. This rocky road version from a "hooked" reader was on a Parkay Margarine package.

½ cup butter or margarine, softened
½ cup brown sugar, packed
1 cup flour
½ cup graham cracker crumbs
2 cups miniature marshmallows
1 (6-ounce) package semisweet chocolate pieces
½ cup chopped walnuts

Beat butter and brown sugar until fluffy. Combine flour and cracker crumbs and add to sugar mixture, mixing well. Press onto bottom of greased 9-inch square pan. Sprinkle with marshmallows, chocolate pieces and walnuts. Bake at 375 degrees 15 to 20 minutes or until golden brown. Cool. Cut into bars. Makes about 2 dozen.

❖

BEVERAGES

There are so many refreshing drinks available to quench our readers' thirsts. The emergence of trattorias and European-style coffee bars next to magazine and newsstands have brought a new audience for coffee-flavored drinks. Angeleno's are famous for ordering "non-fat half-decaf lattes." They also splurge on icy mocha freezes and rich and spicy Thai tea. We've included these and drinks popular in bars such as daiquiris and mai-tais. For those who would like to serve non-alcoholic beverages, there are several punches which are satisfying.

❖

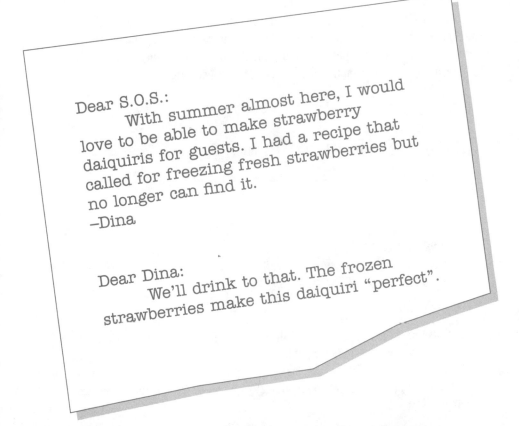

Dear S.O.S.:
    With summer almost here, I would love to be able to make strawberry daiquiris for guests. I had a recipe that called for freezing fresh strawberries but no longer can find it.
—Dina

Dear Dina:
    We'll drink to that. The frozen strawberries make this daiquiri "perfect".

CALIFORNIA SANGRIA

Summer parties often include a California-style sangria made with burgundy, fruit and citrus juice.

1 fifth Burgundy
½ cup brandy
6 tablespoons lemon juice
6 tablespoons pineapple juice
¾ cup orange juice
1 unpeeled apple, sliced
1 unpeeled orange, sliced
1 peach, sliced
Ice cubes
1 (12-ounce) bottle club soda
Orange peel spiral, optional

Combine Burgundy, brandy, lemon, pineapple and orange juices in clear glass pitcher. Add fruit slices. When ready to serve stir in ice cubes and club soda. Garnish pitcher with long orange peel spiral, if wanted. Serve with wooden spoon in pitcher adding a few pieces of fruit for each serving. Makes 4 servings.

❖

CHAMPAGNE WEDDING PUNCH

Here's a traditional–and very easy–champagne punch for a wedding.

1 small orange
2 fifths chablis, chilled
Ice cubes
1 fifth extra dry champagne, chilled

Cut peel of orange into thick spiral, cutting slightly into pulp, leaving attached to orange. Place orange in large pitcher. Pour in chablis and let stand 15 minutes. Add one tray ice cubes and champagne. Detach spiral of peel. Hang spiral on rim of pitcher for decoration. Makes about 2½ quarts or 20 (4-ounce) punch cup servings.

MAI-TAI

Readers returning from Hawaii invariably request a recipe for the popular Mai Tai cocktail served garnished with a vanda orchid, mint leaf, pineapple spear and maraschino cherry.

½ lime
2 teaspoons orgeat syrup
2 teaspoons rock candy syrup
2 teaspoons orange Curaçao
2 tablespoons lemon juice
1 ¼ ounces golden rum
1 ¼ ounces dark rum
Shaved ice
Maraschino cherry, pineapple spear, sprig of mint and
  vanda orchid, optional

Squeeze juice from lime into 13-ounce cocktail glass and drop squeezed lime into glass. Add orgeat syrup, rock candy syrup, orange Curaçao, lemon juice, golden rum and dark rum. Fill glass with shaved ice. Garnish with cherry, pineapple, mint and orchid. Serve with straw. Makes 1 serving.

❖

PERFECT STRAWBERRY-BANANA DAIQUIRI

Bonavista, a revolving cocktail lounge at the Bonaventure Hotel in Los Angeles serves strawberry-banana daiquiris which our readers call "perfect."

1 cup chilled light rum
¾ cup chilled fresh lime juice
¼ cup sugar
2 cups frozen whole strawberries
2 cups chopped bananas

Pour rum and lime juice in blender container. Add sugar, blend to dissolve. Drop frozen berries into blender container, a few at a time, then add bananas blending until smooth. Pour into chilled glasses. Makes 6 servings.

COFFEE LIQUEUR

Readers have told us that this home recipe for coffee liqueur tastes better and costs less than the commercial type.

1 pint distilled water
1 (2-ounce) jar instant coffee
4 cups sugar
1 quart vodka
1 vanilla bean

Bring water to boil in saucepan. Add coffee powder and sugar. Stir until coffee and sugar dissolve. Cool.

Add vodka and pour into 2 (1-liter) bottles. Cut vanilla bean in half and split each half lengthwise before adding to bottles. Cap and let stand one month before serving. Makes 2 liters.

❖

MOCHA FREEZE

This frosty, thick mocha drink is easy to make at home.

2 cups ice cubes or chips
½ cup strong coffee
3 tablespoons half and half
1 cup milk
2 tablespoons chocolate drink mix or to taste

In blender, combine ice, coffee, half and half, milk and chocolate drink mix. Blend until thick and foamy. Serve with straw. Makes 2 servings.

❖

Orange Juliana

We have yet to solve the mystery of a true recipe for Orange Julius, an orange drink sold in Los Angeles. But we and our readers keep trying.

> *½ (6-ounce) can frozen orange juice concentrate*
> *½ cup milk*
> *½ cup water*
> *¼ cup sugar*
> *½ teaspoon vanilla*
> *5 or 6 ice cubes*

Combine orange juice concentrate, milk, water, sugar, vanilla and ice cubes in blender container. Cover and blend until smooth, about 30 seconds. Serve immediately. Makes about 3 cups.

❖

Thai Tea

Thai's moving to Los Angeles in the seventies introduced this incredibly tasty tea to Southern Californians. You'll need to purchase Indochinese tea, which is commonly sold in Asian markets (principally Vietnamese and Chinese) for the proper effect. Sweetened condensed milk used both to sweeten and texture the beverage is a must.

> *8 cups water*
> *6 tablespoons Thai tea leaves*
> *Sugar*
> *Ice cubes*
> *Sweetened condensed milk or half and half*

Bring water to boil. Add tea and steep 5 minutes. Strain and add sugar to taste. Cool, then chill in refrigerator.

To serve, place ice cubes in each of 6 tall glasses. Pour tea over ice to within ½ inch of rim. Fill glasses with milk and stir. Makes 6 servings.

❖

SHERBET PUNCH

This sweet and smooth non-alcoholic punch is a favorite wedding punch. You can vary the flavorings by using any fruit concentrate and complementary sherbet.

½ gallon raspberry sherbet
1 (6-ounce) can frozen lemonade concentrate
6 (28-ounce) bottles ginger ale or lemon-lime carbonated
   beverage, chilled
Berries or fruit pieces, optional

Turn sherbet into large punch bowl and break into chunks. Dilute concentrate according to label directions and add to sherbet. Pour ginger ale into punch bowl and stir lightly. Garnish with fruit, if desired. Makes about 50 servings.

❖

MOCK CHAMPAGNE

Many of our readers, and their guests, have been deceived by this bubbly champagne punch imitation.

⅔ cup sugar
⅔ cup water
1 cup grapefruit juice
½ cup orange juice
3 tablespoons grenadine
1 (28-ounce) bottle ginger ale, chilled

Stir sugar and water over low heat until sugar is dissolved. Bring to boil and boil 10 minutes. Cool. Add sugar syrup to grapefruit and orange juices. Chill thoroughly. Add grenadine and ginger ale just before serving. Makes 1½ quarts or 12 (4-ounce) servings.

❖

DAIRY EGGNOG

Readers who would rather make their own eggnog instead of using the commercial brand always turn to this recipe from our past files.

6 eggs, separated
½ cup sugar
4 cups milk
¼ teaspoon salt
2 cups whipping cream
2 teaspoons vanilla
Freshly ground nutmeg

Lightly beat egg yolks, add ¼ cup sugar and beat thoroughly. Scald milk and stir slowly into yolks. Cook, stirring constantly, over low heat until mixture coats metal spoon. Chill. Several hours before serving, add salt to egg whites and beat until stiff, gradually adding remaining ¼ cup sugar. Fold into custard mixture. Whip cream and fold into eggnog. Add vanilla. Chill several hours then serve sprinkled with nutmeg. Makes about 24 (4-ounce) servings.

❖

GRAB BAG

Relishes, Butters, Sauces, Frostings, Jellies,
Condiments and other good things...

    As you would guess, this final chapter is filled with odds and ends so full of surprises that you'll want to give many of them a try, if only to save a few pennies while having fun. *Mock Devonshire cream* looks and tastes like the real thing bought at gourmet stores. You can make inexpensive biscuit mix, cocoa mix and mayonnaise. The hot fudge sauce is as good as the most expensive and the butters are dense with flavor. The jams and preserves are fragrant with fresh fruit. We've also included hard-to-find recipes such as soda crackers and yogurt-covered nuts.

❖

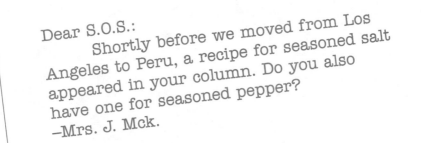

Dear S.O.S.:
    Shortly before we moved from Los Angeles to Peru, a recipe for seasoned salt appeared in your column. Do you also have one for seasoned pepper?
—Mrs. J. Mck.

Dear Mrs. J. Mck:
    Here are both recipes.

APPLE-CIDER BUTTER

This slightly different apple butter owes its rich taste to brown sugar and cider.

4 pound apples
Apple cider
Brown sugar
¼ teaspoon salt
1 teaspoon ground cinnamon
½ teaspoon ground allspice
½ teaspoon ground cloves

Peel, core and slice apples. Measure fruit and place in large kettle. Add equal amount of apple cider and cook until fruit is tender.

Purée cooked fruit in food processor or blender. Measure fruit pulp and place in large kettle. Add half as much brown sugar as pulp. (More may be added if mixture is not sweet enough.) Add salt. Cook, stirring constantly to prevent sticking and scorching, until mixture starts to thicken. Stir in cinnamon, allspice and cloves.

Reduce heat and continue cooking until fruit butter is thick (add more cider if mixture becomes too thick). Test for doneness by pouring small quantity on cold dish. Butter is done when no rim of liquid separates out around edge of butter.

Pour boiling butter into hot, sterilized jars, leaving ¼-inch head space. Adjust caps. Process pints and quarts 10 minutes in boiling water bath. When cool, test for seal. Makes 1½ quarts.

❖

PUMPKIN BUTTER

This mouth-watering spread is requested near Thanksgiving and goes on until the holiday season is over.

1 (1-pound, 13-ounce) can pumpkin
1 tablespoon pumpkin pie spice
1 (1 ¾-ounce) package powdered pectin
4 ½ cups sugar
Household paraffin, melted

Turn pumpkin into large saucepan. Add spice and pectin to pumpkin, mixing well. Place over high heat and stir until mixture comes to hard boil. Stir in sugar at once. Bring to full rolling boil and boil 1 minute, stirring constantly. Remove from heat. Ladle quickly into hot jars. Cover at once with ⅛-inch layer hot paraffin. Makes 7 (8-ounce) glasses.

❖

CRANBERRY BUTTER

Flavored butters beg to be spread on hot breads and muffins. Think about this butter spread on a corn muffin.

1 cup cranberries
½ cup sugar
1 pound unsalted butter, softened

Cook cranberries with sugar about 10 minutes or until berries have popped and mixture thickens, about 10 minutes. Cool. Blend cranberry mixture into butter with wooden spoon. Pack into crocks or molds. Chill. Serve with hot corn sticks, corn bread, muffins or coffeecake. Makes about 3 cups.

❖

BISCUIT MIX

If you use biscuit mix often, you may want to consider making your own.

> *8 cups sifted flour*
> *¼ cup baking powder*
> *4 teaspoons salt*
> *1 cup shortening*

Sift flour with baking powder and salt. Cut in shortening until mixture resembles coarse cornmeal. Cover tightly and store in refrigerator. To make biscuits, measure out 2 cups mix and add ⅔ to ¾ cup milk. Stir dough until it forms ball. Roll or pat out to ¼ to ½ inch thick. Cut biscuits and bake on baking sheet at 450 degrees 10 to 12 minutes. Makes about 8 cups mix.

CHOCOLATE PUDDING MIX

Mothers who frequently serve their children chocolate pudding would benefit from having it made from a homemade mix that costs roughly half of any commercial brand.

1 ½ cups unsweetened cocoa
1 ¼ cups cornstarch
3 cups sugar
5 cups nonfat instant dry milk powder
½ teaspoon salt

Sift cocoa with cornstarch, sugar, dry milk and salt three times. Spoon mix into glass jars or cans. Do not pack down. Keep tightly closed in a cool place. Makes about 10 cups.

CHOCOLATE PUDDING MIX

⅔ cup Chocolate Pudding Mix
2 cups water
2 tablespoons butter or margarine
½ teaspoon vanilla

Measure mix into saucepan. Stir in water and cook and stir over low heat until pudding boils and thickens. Remove from heat and stir in butter and vanilla. Cool. Makes 4 servings.

❖

INSTANT MOCHA COFFEE MIX

Prepare a batch of Instant Mocha Coffee Mix to make inexpensive Vienna or Irish mocha coffees.

> *1 cup instant cocoa mix*
> *$\frac{1}{2}$ cup instant coffee*

Combine cocoa mix and coffee mix until well blended. Store in covered container to use as needed. Use 2 teaspoons mix for each cup serving. Makes 1$\frac{1}{2}$ cups mix.

❖

MAKE YOUR OWN COCOA MIX

Making your own cocoa mix for hot chocolate or flavoring cakes, cookies or pies, will save money.

> *5 cups instant nonfat dry milk powder*
> *$\frac{3}{4}$ cup sugar*
> *$\frac{3}{4}$ cup unsweetened cocoa powder*

Blend nonfat dry milk, sugar and cocoa in paper or plastic bag and store in dry place. Use as needed. Makes 6$\frac{1}{2}$ cups mix.

Note: $\frac{1}{4}$ cup mix for each 1 cup serving hot chocolate made with hot water or milk.

❖

GRANOLA

Granola, once only available in health food stores, can now be found on the breakfast menu of many restaurants.

24 pitted dates
1 pound old-fashioned oatmeal
1 cup shredded coconut, preferably unsweetened
1 cup pine nuts
1 cup shelled sunflower seeds
1 cup wheat germ
½ cup sesame seeds
½ cup honey
½ cup oil

Cut dates into small pieces with kitchen shears. Combine oatmeal, coconut, pine - nuts, sunflower seeds, wheat germ and sesame seeds in large bowl.

Combine honey and oil in saucepan and heat until almost boiling. Stir into oatmeal mixture. Mix well. Spread ⅓ to half of mixture on large shallow baking pan. Bake at 325 degrees 25 minutes, stirring occasionally. Repeat with remaining mixture. When all cereal is baked, stir in dates. Cool and store in tightly covered containers. Serve as breakfast cereal with or without milk. Makes about 1½ pounds.

Note: Pitted prunes and other dried fruits may be substituted for the dates.

❖

EGGLESS MAYONNAISE

We developed this recipe for eggless mayonnaise after safety warnings about raw eggs.

¼ teaspoon paprika
¼ teaspoon dry mustard
Dash red pepper
1 cup nonfat milk
1 teaspoon unflavored gelatin
¼ cup lemon juice

Mix paprika, dry mustard and red pepper with ½ cup nonfat milk. Stir in gelatin. Heat remaining ½ cup nonfat milk and add to gelatin mixture. Stir in lemon juice. Chill in refrigerator until half congealed. Beat until fluffy. Return to refrigerator and chill until firm. Remove and beat once again. Store in covered jar in refrigerator. Stir vigorously before serving. Thin with lemon juice as desired. Makes 1 cup.

❖

LAWRY'S CREAMED HORSERADISH

Simple as it may sound, this creamed horseradish served with prime ribs at the Lawry's Prime Rib restaurant chain in Los Angeles, is as popular today as it was when the request for a recipe first arrived in 1967.

1 cup whipping cream
1 ounce horseradish root, peeled and grated or ground
1 teaspoon seasoned salt
2 or 3 drops hot pepper sauce

Whip cream until soft peaks form. Gradually add horseradish, seasoned salt and hot pepper sauce to taste. Continue whipping until stiff. Refrigerate until ready to serve. Makes 2 cups.

❖

SEASONED SALT

Budget-minded readers often request the recipes for seasoned salt and pepper.

6 tablespoons salt
½ teaspoon dried thyme
½ teaspoon dried marjoram
½ teaspoon garlic salt
1 tablespoon paprika
½ teaspoon curry powder
¼ teaspoon onion powder
¼ teaspoon dried dill weed
½ teaspoon celery seed or salt

Combine spices and stir with wooden spoon to blend. Pack lightly into bottles or jars, cap tightly and store in cool, dry place away from light. Makes about ½ cup.

❖

SEASONED PEPPER

6 tablespoons coarsely ground black pepper
½ teaspoon salt
¼ teaspoon sugar, optional
½ teaspoon dried sweet green pepper
½ teaspoon dried sweet red pepper
½ teaspoon dried finely minced onion
1 teaspoon paprika

Combine seasonings and stir with wooden spoon to blend. Pack lightly into bottles or jars, cap tightly and store in cool dry place away from light. Makes about ½ cup.

❖

FREEZER JAM

Almost any summer fruit or berries can be used to make this easy, no-cook jam that can be frozen indefinitely or stored in the refrigerator up to 3 weeks.

3 pounds peaches, peeled and cored, or 2 quarts fully ripe blackberries,
     boysenberries, loganberries, raspberries or strawberries
6 cups sugar
1 cup water
1 (1 ³/₄-ounce) package powdered fruit pectin.

Grind peeled and cored peaches. Or wash and crush berries. If desired, sieve all or part of berry pulp to remove seeds , if using berries. (There should be about 4 cups fruit.)

Measure fruit adding water, if necessary, to equal 4 cups. Add sugar to fruit and mix well. Let stand 10 minutes.

In small saucepan, combine water and pectin. Cook, stirring, over high heat until mixture comes to full, rolling boil. Boil hard 1 minute, stirring constantly. Add to fruit and sugar mixture. Stir 3 minutes. Ladle into clean glass jars and cover. Allow to stand at room temperature until set. (May take as long as 24 hours.) Store jam in freezer until ready to use. Jam may be kept as long as 3 weeks in refrigerator. Makes 7½ to 8 cups, depending on fruit.

❖

CHAMPAGNE MUSTARD

Sheila Ricci, who operated a tea room in Beverly Hills back in the seventies introduced us to this mustard which is especially wonderful with baked ham.

²/₃ cup champagne vinegar
²/₃ cup dry mustard
3 eggs
³/₄ cup sugar

Combine vinegar and mustard. Beat eggs with sugar. Add egg mixture to mustard mixture in top of double boiler over simmering water, stirring until thick. Refrigerate. Makes 1½ cups.

JOHN SEDLAR'S JALAPEÑO JELLY

John Sedlar, a Los Angeles chef famous for his eclectic southwestern cuisine, uses red wine to mellow this jelly.

10 jalapeño chiles, stemmed, seeded and finely diced
4 sweet red peppers, stemmed, seeded and finely diced
2 cups red wine vinegar
7 cups sugar
1 ½ (6-ounce) packages liquid pectin

Combine chiles, peppers, vinegar and sugar in large heavy saucepan. Simmer 15 minutes. Add pectin and bring to boil. Boil hard 1 minute, stirring constantly. Skim foam if necessary.

Pour into hot, sterilized jars, leaving ¼-inch head space. Adjust caps. Process 5 minutes in boiling water bath. Makes about 4 pints.

❖

EL TORITO SALSA

Readers who know their salsa always ask for this recipe.

2 cups diced tomatoes
½ cup diced onion
1 to 2 tablespoons diced, stemmed and seeded jalapeños
1 tablespoon oil
1 teaspoon white distilled vinegar
1 teaspoon fresh lime juice
½ teaspoon dried Mexican oregano leaves
¼ teaspoon salt
¼ cup finely chopped cilantro

Combine tomatoes, onion, jalapeños, oil, vinegar, lime juice, oregano, salt and cilantro. Makes 4 servings.

❖

GELATIN WHIPPED CREAM

A baker's trick is to add gelatin to whipped cream when frosting cakes for a longer shelf life.

1 teaspoon unflavored gelatin
4 teaspoons cold water
1 cup whipping cream
¼ cup powdered sugar
½ teaspoon vanilla, optional

Sprinkle gelatin over cold water to soften. Place over low heat until gelatin dissolves, stirring occasionally. Remove from heat. Cool slightly. Whip cream until soft peaks form. Add powdered sugar and vanilla. Beat until thickened. Slowly beat in gelatin. Whip at high speed until stiff. Pipe or spread at once. Makes about 2 cups.

❖

MOCK DEVONSHIRE CREAM

You'll never tell the difference when tasting this version of rich Devonshire cream, which is great on scones.

1 (4.6 ounce) package vanilla pudding mix, not instant
3 cups half and half
2 (3-ounce) packages cream cheese, softened

Blend pudding mix with half and half in saucepan. Cook and stir over medium heat until mixture comes to full boil. Remove from heat and pour into bowl. Blend in cream cheese with fork until mixture has small lumps of cheese throughout. Cover and refrigerate. Serve with strawberries or other fruit. Makes 4 cups.

❖

BAKERY-TYPE CREAMY FROSTING

Professional bakers use this creamy frosting to pipe decorations and frost cakes without worry of melting or spoiling.

> *2 tablespoons flour*
> *$\frac{1}{2}$ cup milk*
> *$\frac{1}{2}$ cup sugar*
> *$\frac{1}{4}$ cup margarine, softened*
> *$\frac{1}{4}$ cup shortening*
> *Dash salt*
> *$\frac{1}{2}$ cup powdered sugar*
> *1 teaspoon vanilla*

Mix flour with milk in small saucepan. Cook over low heat until thickened, stirring constantly. Cool.

Cream sugar and margarine with shortening until fluffy. Add salt and cooled flour-milk paste and beat until doubled. Beat in powdered sugar and vanilla. Makes about 1 cup.

Note: Do not substitute butter for margarine.

❖

MARSHMALLOW FROSTING

For many readers this frosting made with marshmallows, brings back memories of grandma's baking.

> *32 marshmallows*
> *$\frac{2}{3}$ cup milk*
> *$\frac{3}{4}$ cup cold firm butter or margarine*
> *1 teaspoon vanilla*

Combine marshmallows and milk. Cook over low heat until marshmallows dissolve. Cool to room temperature, stirring to blend thoroughly.

Cream butter until light and fluffy at medium speed of electric mixer. Continue to beat, gradually adding marshmallow mixture. Add vanilla. Continue beating until mixture is stiff. Makes enough Marshmallow Frosting for two-layer cake.

TUTTI FRUTTI

When readers request a recipe for tutti frutti, crockpot fruit or rumtopf, we know they mean brandied fruit, the kind served over ice cream, angel food or pound cakes, or eaten as a dessert by itself. The summer season is the perfect time to start a pot, to which you can add fruit throughout the year. Any combination of fruit–or even a single type–can start the crockpot going. Keep in mind that brandied fruits make great holiday gifts, too.

1 cup brandy
1 cup whole or halved strawberries
1 cup fresh pineapple chunks
1 cup pitted dark sweet cherries
1 cup red raspberries
1 cup sliced, peeled and pitted apricots
1 cup sliced, peeled and pitted peaches
1 cup currants, optional
7 cups sugar

Use large crock with lid or 3-quart glass jar. Place brandy in jar and add 1 cup fruit of choice and 1 cup sugar. Do not fasten lid tightly. Add each fruit as it comes in season, adding as much sugar as fruit each time. Stir gently occasionally to dissolve sugar but do not crush fruit. Store in cool place. When a sugar is dissolved, secure lid. Fruit will keep indefinitely. Makes about 10 servings.

❖

TRADITIONAL RUM SAUCE

Here's the traditional rum sauce for mincemeat pies, bread pudding, plum pudding and even ice cream.

1 ½ cups sherry, about
1 tablespoon rum extract or rum
1 tablespoon vanilla
1 pound powdered sugar

Combine sherry, rum and vanilla extracts. Gradually add mixture to powdered sugar, blending thoroughly. If too thick add additional sherry. Refrigerate. Serve over ice cream, pound cake or fruit desserts. Makes 2⅔ cups rum sauce.

OLD-FASHIONED HOT FUDGE SAUCE

Those who remember when hot fudge sauce became thick and stringy upon contact with ice cream love this version.

2 (1-ounce) squares unsweetened chocolate
½ cup light corn syrup
Dash salt
½ teaspoon vanilla
½ teaspoon butter or margarine

Melt chocolate in top of double boiler over hot, not boiling water. Add syrup and cook over hot water until chocolate melts and is blended. Add salt, vanilla and butter. Makes about 1 cup.

❖

GUMBO POT PEPPERED PECANS

When readers discovered the peppered pecans used in the dressing for fried chicken salad at the Gumbo Pot in the Farmer's Market, they flipped and requests poured in. They're also great by themselves as a cocktail snack.

½ cup sugar
1 tablespoon kosher salt
1 ½ tablespoons freshly ground black pepper
4 ounces pecan halves

Mix sugar with salt and pepper. Set aside.

Heat cast-iron skillet until hot enough to vaporize water. Shake pecans in skillet 1 minute to release oil. Lightly toast until fragrant. Add half of pepper mixture, shaking pecans constantly. When sugar begins to caramelize, add remaining pepper mixture, shaking pecans constantly. Turn out to cool and separate. Makes 2 cups.

❖

HONEY CRACKLE CORN

Here's a classic, fun-to-make caramel nut corn that's far less expensive than store-bought varieties.

3 quarts freshly popped corn
1 cup blanched slivered almonds
½ cup butter or margarine
1 cup light brown sugar, packed
¼ cup honey
1 teaspoon vanilla

Turn popped corn into large, shallow roasting pan. Sprinkle almonds over corn.

Melt butter in 1-quart saucepan. Stir in sugar and honey. Cook, stirring, over medium heat until mixture comes to boil. Simmer without stirring 5 minutes.

Remove from heat and stir in vanilla. Pour mixture over popped corn and almonds and stir until well mixed. Bake at 250 degrees, stirring every 15 minutes, 1 hour. Cool completely. Break apart and store in tightly covered container. Makes about 3 quarts.

❖

YOGURT-COVERED NUTS

Readers who enjoy making their children's favorite high energy snacks, find these worth the trouble to make at home.

½ cup granulated sugar
1 cup light-brown sugar, packed
½ cup plain yogurt
1 teaspoon vanilla
2 cups walnut or pecan halves

Combine sugars and yogurt in medium saucepan. Cook over medium heat until mixture reaches soft ball stage (about 235 degrees on candy thermometer). Add vanilla and cool until mixture begins to thicken. Add nuts. Stir until nuts are covered. Place on lightly buttered pan to cool. Cut in pieces. Makes about 2½ pounds.

INDEX

NOTES

NOTES

NOTES

NOTES

ABOUT THE AUTHOR

Rose Dosti has been a Los Angeles Times food writer, restaurant reviewer and editor of the food advice column on which *Dear S.O.S.* is based. She is the author of *New California Cuisine*, Tastemaker Award winner *Middle Eastern Cookery*, and *Light Style: The Low-Fat, Low-Cholesterol, Low-Salt Way to Good Food and Health*, which also appears as a column in the Los Angeles Times.

Dear S.O.S.:
    I would appreciate a copy of the "mystery" fudge recipe of a famous brand name candy. It was the best fudge I ever made and regret losing my recipe.
—Connie

Dear Connie:
    No regrets necessary. The recipe is yours once again.